# How Bible Stories Work

# Reading the Bible as Literature

*How Bible Stories Work: A Guided Study of Biblical Narrative*

*Sweeter Than Honey, Richer Than Gold: A Guided Study of Biblical Poetry*

*A Guided Study of the Epistles*

*A Guided Study of the Gospels*

*A Guided Study of Prophecy and Apocalyptic Literature*

*A Guided Study of Wisdom Literature*

READING
THE BIBLE AS
LITERATURE

# How Bible Stories Work

## A GUIDED STUDY
## OF BIBLICAL NARRATIVE

# LELAND RYKEN

WEAVER BOOK
COMPANY

*How Bible Stories Work: A Guided Study of Biblical Narrative*
© 2015 by Leland Ryken

Published by
Weaver Book Company
1190 Summerset Dr.
Wooster, OH 44691
weaverbookcompany.com

Cover design and interior layout: Frank Gutbrod

**Library of Congress Cataloging-in-Publication Data**
Ryken, Leland.

How Bible stories work : a guided study of biblical narrative / Leland Ryken.
pages cm. -- (Reading the Bible as literature)

ISBN 978-1-941337-36-3

1. Bible--Criticism, Narrative. 2. Narration in the Bible. 3. Bible stories.
4. Storytelling--Religious aspects--Christianity. I. Title.
BS521.7.R95 2015
220.6'6--dc23

2015006574

Printed in the United States of America
15 16 17 18 19/ 5 4 3 2 1

# Contents

# *Series Preface*

This series is part of the mission of Weaver Book Company to equip Christians to understand and teach the Bible effectively by giving them reliable tools for handling the biblical text. Within that landscape, the niche that my volumes are designed to fill is the literary approach to the Bible. This has been my scholarly passion for nearly half a century. It is my belief that a literary approach to the Bible is the common reader's friend, in contrast to more specialized types of scholarship on the Bible.

Nonetheless, the literary approach to the Bible needs to be defended against legitimate fears by evangelical Christians, and through the years I have not scorned to clear the territory of misconceptions as part of my defense of a literary analysis of the Bible. In kernel form, my message has been this:

1.  To view the Bible as literature is not a suspect modern idea, nor does it need to imply theological liberalism. The idea of the Bible as literature began with the writers of the Bible, who display literary qualities in their writings and who refer with technical precision to a wide range of literary genres such as psalm, proverb, parable, apocalypse, and many more.

2. Although fiction is a common trait of literature, it is not an essential feature of it. A work of literature can be replete with literary technique and artifice while remaining historically factual.

3. To approach the Bible as literature need not be characterized by viewing the Bible *only* as literature, any more than reading it as history requires us to see only the history of the Bible.

4. When we see literary qualities in the Bible we are not attempting to bring the Bible down to the level of ordinary literature; it is simply an objective statement about the inherent nature of the Bible. The Bible can be trusted to reveal its extraordinary qualities if we approach it with ordinary methods of literary analysis.

To sum up, it would be tragic if we allowed ourselves to be deprived of literary methods of analyzing the Bible by claims that are fallacies.

What, then, does it mean to approach the Bible as literature? A literary study of the Bible should begin where any other approach begins—by accepting as true all that the biblical writers claim about their book. These claims include its inspiration and superintendence by God, its infallibility, its historical truthfulness, its unique power to infiltrate people's lives, and its supreme authority.

With that as a foundation, a literary approach to the Bible is characterized by the following traits:

1. An acknowledgement that the Bible comes to us in a predominantly literary format. In the words of C. S. Lewis, "There is a . . . sense in which the Bible, since it is after all literature, cannot properly be read except as literature; and the different parts of it as the different sorts

of literature they are."[1] The overall format of the Bible is that of an anthology of literature.

2. In keeping with that, a literary approach identifies the genres and other literary forms of the Bible and analyzes individual texts in keeping with those forms. An awareness of literary genres and forms programs how we analyze a biblical text and opens doors into a text that would otherwise remain closed.

3. A literary approach begins with the premise that a work of literature embodies universal human experience. Such truthfulness to human experience is complementary to the tendency of traditional approaches to the Bible to mainly see ideas in it. A literary approach corrects a commonly held fallacy that the Bible is a theology book with proof texts attached.

4. A literary approach to the Bible is ready to grant value to the biblical authors' skill with language and literary technique, seeing these as an added avenue to our enjoyment of the Bible.

5. A literary approach to the Bible takes its humble place alongside the two other main approaches—the theological and the historical. These three domains are established by the biblical writers themselves, who usually combine all three elements in their writings. However, in terms of space, the Bible is a predominantly literary book. Usually the historical and theological material is packaged in literary form.

These traits and methods of literary analysis govern the content of my series of guided studies to the genres of the Bible.

---

1    *Reflections on the Psalms* (New York: Harcourt, Brace & World, 1958), 3.

Although individual books in my series are organized by the leading literary genres that appear in the Bible, I need to highlight that all of these genres have certain traits in common. Literature itself, en masse, makes up a homogenous whole. In fact, we can speak of *literature as a genre* (the title of the opening chapter of a book titled *Kinds of Literature*). The traits that make up literature as a genre will simply be assumed in the volumes in this series. They include the following: universal, recognizable human experience concretely embodied as the subject matter; the packaging of this subject matter in distinctly literary genres; the authors' use of special resources of language that set their writing apart from everyday expository discourse; stylistic excellence and other forms of artistry that are part of the beauty of a work of literature.

What are the advantages that come from applying the methods of literary analysis? In brief, they are as follows: an improved method of interacting with biblical texts in terms of the type of writing that they are; doing justice to the specificity of texts (again because the approach is tailored to the genres of a text); ability to see unifying patterns in a text; relating texts to everyday human experience; enjoyment of the artistic skill of biblical authors.

## Summary

A book needs to be read in keeping with its author's intention. We can see from the Bible itself that it is a thoroughly literary book. God superintended its authors to write a very (though not wholly) literary book. To pay adequate attention to the literary qualities of the Bible not only helps to unlock the meanings of the Bible; it is also a way of honoring the literary intentions of its authors. Surely biblical authors regarded everything that they put into their writing as important. We also need to regard those things as important.

# Introduction

## *Getting the Most Out of Biblical Narrative*

The appeal of stories is universal. In fact, one of the most common human impulses can be summed up in four words: "tell me a story." During the course of a typical day, nearly everyone finds occasion to string together incidents and thereby tell a story. A typical meal with family or friends is an incipient storytelling session. We turn the day's experiences into a story in order to cope with our difficulties and relish our triumphs.

The Bible continuously satisfies the universal human desire for narrative. This was highlighted when Henry R. Luce, founder of *Time* magazine, said in an interview, "*Time* didn't start this emphasis on stories about people; the Bible did." Although the Bible is comprised of dozens of literary genres, the dominant one is narrative. Even the non-narrative parts are placed within an overall story known as universal history and salvation history. A biblical scholar of a bygone era rendered the oft-quoted verdict that "the narrative mode is uniquely important in Christianity," starting with the Bible.[2]

We can assign this dominance of narrative in the Bible to at least three causes. First, it is rooted in the character of God, who is the God who acts. Second, biblical writers are preoccupied with history, and they overwhelmingly want us to know what actually happened. To record what happened is to tell a story. Third, life itself has a narrative quality, being comprised of exactly the same ingredients that stories possess (setting, characters, plot, progression in time, and so forth). The narrative quality of the Bible is part of its truthfulness to life.

The history recorded in the Bible exists on a continuum of which literary narrative is only a part. On one end of the continuum we find the historical impulse to record the facts of what occurred, but nothing more. On the literary end of the continuum we find events, settings, and characters presented in full detail and with artistry, so that we relive the story in our imaginations and relish the storyteller's skill. The historical material of the Bible covers the entire continuum. The more fully a historical account is presented, the more amenable it is to the methods of narrative analysis that I present in this book.

For this guided study I have of course chosen fully literary narrative. Within that category, the guided study format has required that I select brief narratives, not long ones like the books of Ruth and Esther or the stories of Abraham, Jacob, and Isaac in Genesis (though I have selected episodes from those longer narratives). I do not want this to conceal that the methods of analysis that I propound in this book are exactly the right ones to use with long biblical narratives as well as brief ones.

---

2    Amos N. Wilder, *Early Christian Rhetoric: The Language of the Gospel* (Cambridge: Harvard University Press, 1971), 56.

When compared to stories universally, the stories of the Bible are a combination of the familiar and the unique. We should note the following traits as being distinctive to the Bible. First, the preoccupation with history rather than fictional stories like Homer's *Odyssey* or Shakespeare's tragedies and comedies sets biblical narrative apart. In keeping with the authors' intention to stick with the facts, the storytellers of the Bible generally (but not without exception) write in a spare, unembellished style. Their preference is for the brief narrative unit (even though these brief units might be strung together to form a composite long story).

The presence of God as a character and supernatural events in most of the stories is another thing that makes them read differently from stories that we ordinarily read. As an extension of that, the pervasive religious quality of the Bible's stories makes them different from stories generally. We can accurately say of the Bible that it is a divine story that is also a human story; we would only rarely say that of other stories. We can also profitably reverse the formula: the story of the Bible is a human story that is also a divine story. John Calvin was right when he said that true knowledge consists of two things—knowledge of God and knowledge of ourselves (that is, people). The stories of the Bible give us those two things.

A summary statement may be allowed to Erich Auerbach, a literary scholar who wrote a famous essay comparing storytelling technique in Homer and the Bible (for which he chose the story of Abraham's offering of Isaac). Regarding the biblical writers, Auerbach writes, "Their religious intent involves an absolute claim to historical truth. . . . The Bible's claim to truth is not only far more urgent than Homer's, it is tyrannical—it excludes all other claims. . . . The Scripture stories do not, like Homer's, court our favor" but instead "seek to subject us."[3]

---

3  "Odysseus' Scar," in *Mimesis: The Representation of Reality in Western Literature* (Princeton: Princeton University Press, 1953), 14–15.

However, along with these distinctive and sometimes unique features of biblical narrative, the stories of the Bible also share the common techniques of storytelling that have been used by all storytellers from time immemorial. All stories are comprised of setting, character, and plot. All storytellers use such narrative devices as dramatic irony and foreshadowing. All stories are built on the paradigm of plot conflict moving to resolution. Techniques of characterization are the same in the book of Genesis and the novels of Charles Dickens. A lot of harm has been done to people's ability to interpret the stories of the Bible by the tendency of traditional approaches to seal the Bible off in a world of its own.

In this book I have not drawn connections between the stories of the Bible and the familiar stories of English and American literature, but I want my readers not to suppress the correspondences that they see between the stories of the Bible and stories universally. We will see more in the stories of the Bible, and we will handle them better, if we apply what we know about stories elsewhere to the stories of the Bible.

A final preliminary is to note that while stories are stories and not essays with logical development of ideas, there is a discourse level to any serious narrative. A good story does, indeed, entertain us, and it embodies human experience in such a way as to lead us to relive it along with the characters in the story. But a story is also intended by the author to convey a message. Further, this message can at some point be formulated as ideas. The literary term for such ideas is *themes* (generalizations about life).

At one level, a storyteller tells us *about* settings, characters, and events. But fiction writer Flannery O'Connor made the provocative statement that a storyteller speaks *"with* character and action, not *about* character and action."[4] If this is so, *about what* do

---

4    *Mystery and Manners*, ed. Sally and Robert Fitzgerald (New York: Farrar, Straus, & Giroux, 1957), 76.

storytellers speak by means of character and action? The answer: life, reality, truth.

## Summary

Because we read the stories of Bible for edification, we tend over-whelmingly to place them into a category all by themselves. The first step toward a literary approach to the stories of the Bible is to apply all that we know about stories generally. A story needs to be read and analyzed as a story. The stories of the Bible are genuine stories, not something else. They can be trusted to reveal their unique religious qualities if we apply ordinary methods of narrative analysis to them. A literary approach will also reveal how skilled the storytellers of the Bible were at their craft.

# The Subject of Every Story

## The Embodiment of Universal Human Experience

A story has two components known as form and content. While the former is naturally the emphasis of narrative analysis, I have chosen to devote my first chapter to the often overlooked subject of content.

I immediately need to guard myself against possible misunderstanding by acknowledging that in the long run form and content cannot be separated, and that there is no content without the form in which it is embodied. Despite this, it is helpful sometimes to distinguish between form and content.

It is a truism that the subject of literature (whatever the genre) is universal human experience, concretely embodied. While this applies to all literature, it is particularly important for narrative. For one thing, stories more obviously than other genres embody human experience.

Second, unless we have a firm grasp on the experiential nature of stories, we will not see their relevance to life. In regard to the stories of the Bible, traditional approaches have tended to short circuit the fullness of the stories by quickly reducing them to a set of ideas. There is a whole further type of truth beyond the ideational, and it is this other type of truth that is the particular specialty of literature. We can accurately call it truthfulness to human experience and reality.

Drawing an analogy between a photograph and a work of literature will clarify this. A photograph puts a picture of life before us. It prompts us to stare at the photographer's "slice of life." As we stare at it, we come to see the selected sphere of life with heightened clarity. This is true of literature as well. The knowledge that literature imparts is knowledge in the form of right seeing.

## How to See Universal Human Experience in Bible Stories

The best methodology for seeing recognizable human experience in the stories of the Bible is simply the conviction *that* the stories embody familiar human experience. If we are committed to the idea that the story of Jacob (for example) is filled with the experiences of everyday life, we will be able to see and name them.

But a few time-honored methods will help the process of seeing ourselves and our experiences in the stories of the Bible. One of them is the concept of building bridges between the ancient biblical story and our own world. "Bridging the gap" is the familiar term for this process. The gap between ourselves and the stories of the Bible requires us to take a two-way journey. First we need to travel from our own time and place to the world of the story. Paradoxically, the more thoroughly we immerse ourselves in the world of the ancient text, the more likely we are to see recognizable human experience in it.

After we have traveled to the world of the story and lived in it, we need to make a return trip. When we do so, we bridge the gap. The full range of familiar experience is the menu of possible links between the story and our own experience. What is particularly required is the ability to name the experiences of the biblical story in the terms with which we are familiar.

An additional piece of information will aid the process. We need to grasp the difference between literary discourse and expository discourse. Expository discourse is informational and explanatory. It is the language in which we conduct most of our everyday business. A textbook and a news story are examples of expository discourse.

By contrast, literary discourse aims to embody and "image forth" human experience. While expository discourse relies on generalizations, abstraction, and accumulation of facts, literary discourse uses a range of techniques to incarnate human experience as concretely as possible. With literature we do not assimilate facts and ideas but vicariously relive the experiences that the author places before us.

It may appear that we have strayed from the topic of finding recognizable human experience in the stories of the Bible, but we have not. The reason we can find an abundance of universal human experience in the stories of the Bible is that the storyteller has incarnated and embodied the content of the story in pictures, images, characters, and events. It is a truism that history books and the daily news tell us what *happened*, whereas literature tells us what *happens*. American poet Ezra Pound famously quipped that "literature is news that *stays* news." The permanence of literature comes from an author's concrete portrayal of human experience.

## Familiar Human Experience in the Story of Babel (Genesis 11:1–9)

Contrary to what we might think, ancient or primitive literature like the book of Genesis and classical mythology has an uncanny ability to embody universal human experiences that, if viewed in a certain way, are as up to date as the daily newspaper:

¹Now the whole earth had one language and the same words. ²And as people migrated from the east, they found a plain in the land of Shinar and settled there. ³And they said to one another, "Come, let us make bricks, and burn them thoroughly." And they had brick for stone, and bitumen for mortar. ⁴Then they said, "Come, let us build ourselves a city and a tower with its top in the heavens, and let us make a name for ourselves, lest we be dispersed over the face of the whole earth." ⁵And the LORD came down to see the city and the tower, which the children of man had built. ⁶And the LORD said, "Behold, they are one people, and they have all one language, and this is only the beginning of what they will do. And nothing that they propose to do will now be impossible for them. ⁷Come, let us go down and there confuse their language, so that they may not understand one another's speech." ⁸So the LORD dispersed them from there over the face of all the earth, and they left off building the city. ⁹Therefore its name was called Babel, because there the LORD confused the language of all the earth. And from there the LORD dispersed them over the face of all the earth.

We can profitably begin with a bit of context. The first eleven chapters of Genesis are primeval history—so far back at the dawn of human life on earth that it is in some sense before ordinary history (hence known as prehistory). The story patterns in these chapters are elemental and simplified. We might think that such stories are unlikely candidates to yield pictures of universal, recognizable human experience. If we can find everyday human experience in these stories, we should be able to find it anywhere.

Seeing our own life and times in the story of the Tower of Babel starts by journeying to the world of the story and immersing ourselves in it. We cannot know with certainty what the tower looked like or literally was, but for purposes of the meaning of this story any tall tower that we personally imagine will be sufficient. Building the tower was a gesture of aspiration toward deity. The project involved a whole civilization in its conceptualizing and then its construction. It was a product of human ingenuity and technology. Its goal was social unity, based partly on a single language.

All of these things constitute the first half of the story. The second half narrates the defeat of these things. The keynotes are diversity of language, confusion, dispersal of population, abandonment of the building project, and a divided human race.

Even in these broad strokes we can catch a certain modern spirit in the story. But we can zoom in much more closely, and when we do, we are left feeling that we can hardly imagine a story (even a much longer one) that captures so much of our own civilization than this one. I have listed recognizable human experiences below and will leave it to my readers to correlate those experiences with details in the text:

- individual and communal aspiration
- the urge for human fame and achievement
- utopian zeal and dreams
- a spirit of independence
- self-reliance and self-sufficiency
- technology and faith in what it can achieve
- the collective pride of the human race
- the urge for permanence
- the urge for material power
- the city as the locus of human civilization
- human inventiveness and creativity
- social cooperation, based on shared dreams and a single language

- architectural feats
- communal idolatry (finding security in a substitute deity)
- linguistic division among people groups
- the abandonment of hopes and dreams

Later in this book I will explore the discourse level of biblical stories (the ways in which the narrative details embody a message). The key to that element of this story is that God judges and thwarts the human enterprise represented by the Tower of Babel. This story tells us about a failed experiment in living on a grand scale.

But we should not be in a hurry to get to the abstract (propositional) themes of the story. Truthfulness to life is an important part of the truth of this story. This story offers us knowledge in the form of right seeing. To know that God disapproves of the qualities represented by the building project is a platitude—not therefore unimportant or to be scorned, but a platitude nonetheless. The freshness of vision that this story provides is to be found in its projection onto a situation remote from us of the very things that are going on all around us. Thus distanced and simplified, these things stand out luminous before us. Stories (including those in the Bible) function by first removing us from our own time and place and then (when we reflect and analyze) sending us back to our own world with a sharper sense of understanding.

## LEARNING BY DOING

The story of Cain (Gen. 4:1–16) takes us even farther back in human history than the story of the Tower of Babel does. Yet it is hard to find any story in the world that captures so much familiar human experience per line as this story. American novelist John

Steinbeck was so impressed by the universal aspect of the story that he wrote as follows about it: "I think this is the best-known story in the world because it is everybody's story. I think it is the symbol story of the human soul. . . . This old and terrible story is important because it is a chart of the soul" (*East of Eden*, ch. 22).

Here are tips to guide your analysis of universal human experience in the story of Cain:

- Work your way through the story in sequence from beginning to end.
- For every new piece of data that the story puts before you, ponder whether you are looking at something familiar.
- Some of the experiences are global in the sense of extending to the whole story. For example, the overall story embodies the thoroughly recognizable experience of the destructiveness that comes from unchecked evil in one's life.
- Other experiences are embodied in localized details of the story, such as Cain's self-pity when God announces punishment.
- It is impossible to discuss universal human experience in a story without thinking in terms of archetypes. Archetypes are the recurrent plot motifs, character types, and images or settings that recur throughout literature and life. Examples are the problem child, the family farm as the setting for action, and crime and punishment.
- Do not overlook literary categories, since they, too, are familiar experiences to us. Examples are murder story and detective story.
- An important part of bridging the gap is phrasing the issue in terms of your own experience. For example, this

story looks a lot closer to the daily news if we use the label "domestic violence."

With the head start represented by the foregoing tips, you should be able to come up with a list of twenty recognizable human experiences in the sixteen verses that make up this story. With a little creativity, the list can grow to thirty. If you come up short, enlist the help of one or two friends or family members.

¹Now Adam knew Eve his wife, and she conceived and bore Cain, saying, "I have gotten a man with the help of the LORD." ²And again, she bore his brother Abel. Now Abel was a keeper of sheep, and Cain a worker of the ground. ³In the course of time Cain brought to the LORD an offering of the fruit of the ground, ⁴and Abel also brought of the firstborn of his flock and of their fat portions. And the LORD had regard for Abel and his offering, ⁵but for Cain and his offering he had no regard. So Cain was very angry, and his face fell. ⁶The LORD said to Cain, "Why are you angry, and why has your face fallen? ⁷If you do well, will you not be accepted? And if you do not do well, sin is crouching at the door. Its desire is for you, but you must rule over it."

⁸Cain spoke to Abel his brother. And when they were in the field, Cain rose up against his brother Abel and killed him. ⁹Then the LORD said to Cain, "Where is Abel your brother?" He said, "I do not know; am I my brother's keeper?" ¹⁰And the LORD said, "What have you done? The voice of your brother's blood is crying to me from the ground. ¹¹And now you are cursed from the ground, which has opened its mouth to receive your brother's blood from

your hand. [12]When you work the ground, it shall no longer yield to you its strength. You shall be a fugitive and a wanderer on the earth." [13]Cain said to the LORD, "My punishment is greater than I can bear. [14]Behold, you have driven me today away from the ground, and from your face I shall be hidden. I shall be a fugitive and a wanderer on the earth, and whoever finds me will kill me." [15]Then the LORD said to him, "Not so! If anyone kills Cain, vengeance shall be taken on him sevenfold." And the LORD put a mark on Cain, lest any who found him should attack him. [16]Then Cain went away from the presence of the LORD and settled in the land of Nod, east of Eden.

## Final Thoughts on Human Experience as the Subject of Stories

How important is the concept that the subject of stories is universal human experience concretely embodied? It is crucial. People who never see the point of literature are the ones who have never developed the knack of seeing real life in it. Without that connection, it is hard to see the relevance of literature, which becomes a diversion and nothing more. The religious reverence that people have toward the Bible only partly negates this common situation.

For many of my readers, the new idea that I have put on the table is the concept of truthfulness to life as an additional category of truth beyond ideas that are true. I can imagine that someone might feel that ideas are a sufficient type of truth. This view is easily refuted. If ideas are all that matter, the writers of the Bible could have given us a list of ideas. Instead they gave us a book that is predominantly *more* than ideas—stories, for example, and poems made out of images and figures of speech.

Compared to expository writing that gives us only facts or ideas, stories always contain what we might call "excess baggage." Whereas history tells us what happened, a literary narrative fleshes out *how* it happened—not simply by accumulating details but by getting us to relive the events with the characters who were present, usually in the order in which the events unfolded. Truth is experiential as well as ideational. The "excess baggage" beyond facts and ideas that stories include is the added dimension that literature supplies. The ideas in a story do not require this extra material, but the literary dimension does.

We are touching here on the difference between expository (informational and explanatory) writing and literary writing. Teachers of literature and writing courses belabor the point that the task of literature is to *show* rather than *tell*. To show means to embody in concrete images (including the settings, characters, and actions in a story); to tell means to explain and generalize (as in an essay or news report). The same distinction is sometimes expressed by the formulas that literature *enacts* rather than *summarizes*. The command "you shall not murder" is an example of expository discourse. The story of Cain's murder of Abel incarnates that truth in a story that does not use the word "murder" and does not explicitly command us to refrain from it. The command *tells* the truth; the story *shows* the truth. Another dichotomy is to say that literature gives the example rather than the precept (or, even if it also states the precept, its main business is to flesh it out with an example).

## Summary

Literature is life. The truthfulness that it imparts to us is especially truthfulness to human experience and reality. The stories in the Bible are partly *mirrors* in which we see ourselves and partly *windows* through which we observe life around us. In both cases, the knowledge that Bible stories convey is partly knowledge in the form of seeing life accurately.

# 2

# Setting in Bible Stories

## Seeing the Particulars

Of the three elements that make up stories, setting is the neglected one in many people's reading and analysis of stories. This is regrettable, since analysis of setting greatly enriches our experience of a Bible story, and in addition it is an enjoyable exercise to ferret out the ways in which setting enters a story. Whenever the analysis of setting starts to look like no more than a literary exercise, we can bring the enterprise back into focus by reminding ourselves that the goal of inductive Bible study is to look closely at a text. Exploring the ways in which setting enters a story is an excellent way of looking closely at a Bible story.

## Toward a Definition of Setting

Setting should be given a broad definition. It is anything having to do with *where* an event happens or a character is found. But we can expand the concept of setting along the lines of Aristotle's term "spectacle" in his discussion of the six elements that make up a drama. By spectacle Aristotle meant anything that we visualize, such as a character's clothing or the positioning of characters in relation to each other.

Biblical storytellers consistently include such spatial and visual details. In Acts 12: 21 we read, "On an appointed day Herod put on his royal robes, took his seat upon the throne, and delivered an oration to them." Does it make any difference what Herod was wearing and where he sat? Yes, it mattered to the biblical author and to the people who were present at the event, and it needs to matter to us. (If you read the entire story in Acts 12, you will see that these things mattered to God too.)

We can give an even wider scope to the concept of setting than simply physical place and visual detail. Setting can be temporal, for example, encompassing the time of day or time of year. If a biblical storyteller says that "Isaac went out to meditate in the field toward evening" (Gen. 24:63), we can rest assured that we are meant to make something of both the physical place and time of day.

Setting can also be cultural, consisting of such things as the attitudes, beliefs, and customs that prevail in the world within which a story unfolds. Related to that, we also speak of a *historical setting*, which includes the practices, technology, and lifestyle of people living in a specific historical era. Additionally, *geography* can function as a setting in stories, and we should note in this regard that the storytellers of the Bible frequently include geographic place names. For example, when we read that the king "placed in Bethel the priests of the high places that he had made" (1 Kings 12:32), the place name Bethel has important associations in the historical era being described, and in the cultural situation that prevailed, high places denoted a place of idol worship.

Extending the concept of setting in another direction, we also need to be aware that settings in stories almost always take on symbolic overtones. They begin as literal and physical places, but gradually they accrue implied emotional and conceptual meanings. At the very least, they are positive or negative in association. Additionally, a setting often evokes an atmosphere—of danger, for example, or security, or abundance. In the story of the rescue of Lot from Sodom (Gen. 19), the city of Sodom is not only a physical place but a moral monstrosity, and we can scarcely name it without being aware of God's judgment against the evils that it represented.

## How Setting Functions in a Story

The primary function of setting in a story is to provide a fit container for the characters and events that exist within it. Literary scholars have come up with two complementary ways of viewing this situation. One is to speak of a setting as something that *enables* the action that occurs within it. Thus in Ruth 2, the setting of a grain field at harvest time enables the events that happen on the first meeting of Ruth and Boaz—their encounter, their conversation, Ruth's display of industriousness, Boaz's generosity, and Boaz's extending of love tokens to Ruth.

With other stories, the right formula is not that of enabling but rather the idea of *correspondence.* The idea here is that a setting is a fit container for the action, so that we look for connections or correlations between the setting and the actions and characters that exist within it. A good avenue toward seeing this connection is to ask why we would expect an event or character to be present in a given setting. Often the setting is *an extension* of a character or event. For example, we read regarding a demon-possessed man whom Jesus healed that "for a long time [he] had worn no clothes, and he had not lived in a house but among the tombs" (Luke 8:27). Both the disheveled appearance and the tombs are an extension of the man's disordered state.

Related to settings as enabling an action and corresponding to characters and events is the *symbolism* that we are expected to attach to settings in the stories of the Bible. When King Hezekiah received a threatening letter from the Assyrian king Sennacherib, he took the letter to "the house of the LORD, and spread it before the LORD" (Isa. 37:14). Hezekiah could have spread the letter before God anywhere, so we need to explore what was special about the temple, and as we do so, we are led to explore what the temple symbolized or represented to the Old Testament believer.

To sum up, at an interpretive level, settings serve three overlapping functions in a story: they enable the events that happen in them, they serve as a container for and extension of characters and events, and they take on symbolic overtones. We do not need to agonize over which of these three frameworks to use; usually one of them just seems the best one to use in a specific situation.

In addition to the interpretive functions noted above, we should not overlook the obvious: at a literal level, settings are part of the vividness that makes a story come alive in our imaginations. The goal of any storyteller is to lead us vicariously to relive an event. Settings play a crucial role in that enterprise.

## How to Discover Setting in a Story

The methodology for uncovering the presence of setting in a story is both global (dealing with big effects) and local (specific instances of setting). Global analysis takes a birds' eye view of the story and notices the obvious aspects of setting—a rural world of nature in Genesis, for example, or an idealized farming world for the book of Ruth, or the corrupt city in the story of Sodom and Gomorrah. Moving a step in a more specific direction, we note (1) places where setting takes on symbolic significance and (2) ways in which it enables or corresponds to the action that occurs within it.

In addition to overriding observations like these, though, if we want to fully get inside a Bible story, we need to work our way through it verse by verse, noting every instance of setting and analyzing how it contributes to characters and action. The payoffs are huge. We are unlikely to see how pervasive setting is unless we get the word "scene" into the mix, in two ways: a scene of _____ (of terror, of conflict, of encounter, etc.), or a _____ scene (a street scene, a murder scene, a worship scene). Once we start to apply these two formulas, the scoreboard lights up (as seen below).

To sum up, fiction writer Elizabeth Bowen famously said about the role of place in literature that "nothing can happen nowhere." We tend to minimize this until we go through a Bible story verse by verse and name the places where setting emerges, along with how those details of setting contribute to the story and its message. The following analysis of setting in the story of Cain illustrates these things.

## Setting in the Story of Cain (Genesis 4:1–16)

[1]Now Adam knew Eve his wife, and she conceived and bore Cain, saying, "I have gotten a man with the help of the LORD." [2]And again, she bore his brother Abel. Now Abel was a keeper of sheep, and Cain a worker of the ground. [3]In the course of time Cain brought to the LORD an offering of the fruit of the ground, [4]and Abel also brought of the firstborn of his flock and of their fat portions. And the LORD had regard for Abel and his offering, [5]but for Cain and his offering he had no regard. So Cain was very angry, and his face fell. [6]The LORD said to Cain, "Why are you angry, and why has your face fallen? [7]If you do well, will you not be accepted? And if you do not do well, sin is crouching at the door. Its desire is for you, but you must rule over it."

[8]Cain spoke to Abel his brother. And when they were in the field, Cain rose up against his brother Abel and killed him. [9]Then the LORD said to Cain, "Where is Abel your brother?" He said, "I do not know; am I my brother's keeper?" [10]And the LORD said, "What have you done? The voice of your brother's blood is crying to me from the ground. [11]And now you are cursed from the ground, which has opened its mouth to receive your brother's blood from your hand. [12]When you work the ground, it shall no longer yield to you its strength. You shall be a fugitive and a wanderer on the earth." [13]Cain said to the LORD, "My punishment is greater than I can bear. [14]Behold, you have driven me today away from the ground, and from your face I shall be hidden. I shall be a fugitive and a wanderer on the earth, and whoever finds me will kill me." [15]Then the LORD said to him, "Not so! If anyone kills Cain, vengeance shall be taken on him sevenfold." And the LORD put a mark on Cain, lest any who found him should attack him. [16]Then Cain went away from the presence of the LORD and settled in the land of Nod, east of Eden.

We can start at a global level. The setting is domestic and familial, first of all. The action occurs on the family farm. From start to finish, moreover, we move in a religious world that includes God as an active character in the story. As is common in the Bible, the setting is an elemental world of farming, shepherding, sacrifice, harvest, ground, and earth. With a little analysis, we can see how these settings enable the action—farming for harvest, place of worship for sacrifice, an unlocalized field for murder, the undesignated earth as the place where Cain lives as a fugitive exiled from God.

But setting is also specific, as the following tabulation shows:

- verses 1–2: a sex scene, two birth scenes, a work scene
- verses 3–4: a worship scene
- verse 5: a scene of rejection
- verses 6–7: a scene of encounter, which is also a counseling scene; additionally, in v. 7 the speech of God implies that Cain's heart or soul is the setting for the ultimate action of the story (a spiritual setting)
- verse 8: murder scene
- verses 9–12: arrest scene, scene of accusation, sentencing scene
- verses 13–14: scene of protest
- verse 15: scene of protection
- verse 16: scene of exile and wandering

Nothing can happen nowhere. Every verse has a corresponding setting that either enables an action or is a part of it. It may appear that the labels that I have listed merely name actions, but this is misleading. As we end the story, we do not feel that we have only witnessed actions but rather that we have visited a sequence of settings or scenes. Furthermore, when we label the data using terms of setting, we start to visualize the actions as occurring in space and time. We infer a lot that would otherwise be dormant.

## LEARNING BY DOING

With the foregoing analysis of setting in the story of Cain serving as a model, you are hereby asked to analyze the presence and role of setting in the story of Ruth and Boaz as recorded in Ruth 2. Here is a checklist to aid your analysis:

- the big, global settings in the story, along with how these settings enable the action that occurs in the chapter

- symbolic overtones of these global settings
- detailed (even verse-by-verse) analysis, using the formulas _____ scene or scene of

  _____
- inferred positioning of characters in a setting or in relation to each other

The more we visualize in a story, the richer will be our experience of it.

### RUTH 2

[1] Now Naomi had a relative of her husband's, a worthy man of the clan of Elimelech, whose name was Boaz. [2] And Ruth the Moabite said to Naomi, "Let me go to the field and glean among the ears of grain after him in whose sight I shall find favor." And she said to her, "Go, my daughter." [3] So she set out and went and gleaned in the field after the reapers, and she happened to come to the part of the field belonging to Boaz, who was of the clan of Elimelech. [4] And behold, Boaz came from Bethlehem. And he said to the reapers, "The LORD be with you!" And they answered, "The LORD bless you." [5] Then Boaz said to his young man who was in charge of the reapers, "Whose young woman is this?" [6] And the servant who was in charge of the reapers answered, "She is the young Moabite woman, who came back with Naomi from the country of Moab. [7] She said, 'Please let me glean and gather among the sheaves after the reapers.' So she came, and she has continued from early morning until now, except for a short rest."

[8] Then Boaz said to Ruth, "Now, listen, my daughter, do not go to glean in another field or leave this one, but

keep close to my young women. [9]Let your eyes be on the field that they are reaping, and go after them. Have I not charged the young men not to touch you? And when you are thirsty, go to the vessels and drink what the young men have drawn." [10]Then she fell on her face, bowing to the ground, and said to him, "Why have I found favor in your eyes, that you should take notice of me, since I am a foreigner?" [11]But Boaz answered her, "All that you have done for your mother-in-law since the death of your husband has been fully told to me, and how you left your father and mother and your native land and came to a people that you did not know before. [12]The LORD repay you for what you have done, and a full reward be given you by the LORD, the God of Israel, under whose wings you have come to take refuge!" [13]Then she said, "I have found favor in your eyes, my lord, for you have comforted me and spoken kindly to your servant, though I am not one of your servants."

[14]And at mealtime Boaz said to her, "Come here and eat some bread and dip your morsel in the wine." So she sat beside the reapers, and he passed to her roasted grain. And she ate until she was satisfied, and she had some left over. [15]When she rose to glean, Boaz instructed his young men, saying, "Let her glean even among the sheaves, and do not reproach her. [16]And also pull out some from the bundles for her and leave it for her to glean, and do not rebuke her."

[17]So she gleaned in the field until evening. Then she beat out what she had gleaned, and it was about an ephah of barley. [18]And she took it up and went into the city.

Her mother-in-law saw what she had gleaned. She also brought out and gave her what food she had left over after being satisfied. [19]And her mother-in-law said to her, "Where did you glean today? And where have you worked? Blessed be the man who took notice of you." So she told her mother-in-law with whom she had worked and said, "The man's name with whom I worked today is Boaz." [20]And Naomi said to her daughter-in-law, "May he be blessed by the LORD, whose kindness has not forsaken the living or the dead!" Naomi also said to her, "The man is a close relative of ours, one of our redeemers." [21]And Ruth the Moabite said, "Besides, he said to me, 'You shall keep close by my young men until they have finished all my harvest.'" [22]And Naomi said to Ruth, her daughter-in-law, "It is good, my daughter, that you go out with his young women, lest in another field you be assaulted." [23]So she kept close to the young women of Boaz, gleaning until the end of the barley and wheat harvests. And she lived with her mother-in-law.

## More Thoughts on Setting in Biblical Narrative

The foregoing discussion of how setting functions in Bible stories has broken the overall subject into its constituent parts (setting as enabler of action, as a fit container that correlates with characters and events that exist inside it, and as symbol). This degree of specificity yields the best results. However, if the process ever starts to seem burdensome, there is a simple procedure that is easy to apply: *pay close attention to every detail of setting that a storyteller puts into a story and decide how that detail contributes to the story.*

Many Bible readers resist paying close attention to setting in the stories of the Bible because they have never been encouraged to analyze the pervasive presence of setting in a story and its functions. But that is a weak reason not to exert the effort required to perform the kind of analysis that this chapter has laid out. Analysis of setting enhances our enjoyment of a story and opens doors to our understanding that remain closed if we do not analyze the role of setting.

Additionally, since the goal of Bible study is to see what is actually present in a biblical text, anything that gets us to stare at the text is useful. Fiction writer Flannery O'Connor once wrote that a writer should never be afraid of staring (that is, staring at life and human experience). Literary critics apply that statement to readers as well: a reader should never be afraid of staring. Scrutinizing the settings in a Bible story is one of the more enjoyable and enlightening ways of staring at a text.

In staring at a text, it is entirely appropriate to exercise our imaginations as we put details from a biblical story into a visualized scene. In the story of Abraham's offering of Isaac, we read, "God tested Abraham and said to him, 'Abraham!' And he said, 'Here am I'" (Gen. 22:1). That looks like mere plot summary until a literary scholar does the following with it: "The two speakers are not on the same level: if we conceive of Abraham in the foreground, where it might be possible to picture him as prostrate or kneeling or bowing with outspread arms or gazing upward, God is not there too: Abraham's words and gestures are directed toward the depths of the picture or upward, but in any case the undetermined, dark place from which the voice comes to him is not in the foreground."[5] When the data is handled in this way, plot summary becomes transformed into a visualized scene.

---

5    Erich Auerbach, *Mimesis: The Representation of Reality in Western Literature* (Princeton: Princeton University Press, 1953), 8.

There is one more aspect to setting in stories that yields rich dividends of a different sort. Whenever we sit down to read a story, we enter a whole world of the imagination. This world has its own distinctive traits. Naming the features of this narrative world prompts us to analyze the story as a whole and alerts us to the author's worldview and moral vision.

If we apply this to the story of Cain as an example, it yields something like the following. The world of the story is a domestic world in which all of the action occurs within a family setting. This hints at the importance and primacy of the family as a social unit in this particular story. The world of the story is also a religious world in which God is the ultimate being and in which the important thing about characters and their actions is how they relate to God. Additionally, the world of the story is one in which people are placed in situations that test them and require them to choose between good and evil.

The primary function of analyzing the narrative world of a story in this way is that it supplies a good way of viewing the story as a whole. In addition to thus serving as a unifying framework for a story, it is an index to the values and worldview of a story.

## Summary

Setting is one of three ingredients that make up every story. It is no less important than character and plot. In fact, it enables the characters and plot to exist. To see how pervasive setting is in a biblical story, we need to move beyond the obvious setting in a story (such as a prison in the story of Peter's rescue [Acts 12:6–11]) to more specific ones like a waking scene (v. 7) and scene of dressing (v. 8). Surprising as it may seem, looking at the details of setting has a knack for taking us inside a Bible story, while attention to more obvious features like character and plot may leave us at a more surface level.

# 3

# *Characterization in Bible Stories (Part 1)*

## *How Writers Do It*

Characters are one of three ingredients in stories. The actual methodology for getting to know the characters in Bible stories appears in the next chapter. But that does not make this chapter expendable. What I cover in this chapter is foundational for describing and interpreting characters in the stories of the Bible. We will do a better job of dealing with characters in biblical narrative if we possess the information that I cover in this chapter. The specific focus of this chapter is the author's role in characterization—how storytellers perform their feats of characterization.

The first thing that we need to grasp is that characterization in stories is the product of the storyteller's craft and composition. Real life presented biblical authors with *the materials for* their characters, but the characters as they exist in the stories are the result of many choices on the part of the authors. Real life does not give us literary characters; it gives us the materials for creating literary characters through a process of selectivity of material and massaging of that material once it is selected.

The quickest way to convince yourself of this is to try your hand at storytelling. Just select an event from the past week that happened to you, your family, or an acquaintance. Turn the event into a one-page narrative. Do not use the first-person "I" point of view but the third-person point of view ("he," "she," "they"). When faced with this assignment, the overwhelming majority of people produce a story that is nearly all plot (action) and is virtually devoid of characterization. Such characters as appear are what literary critics call *functional characters*—agents necessary to the action but not having a meaningful identity in themselves.

If we put action stories like these alongside the stories of the Bible with their gallery of memorable characters, it is obvious that the storytellers of the Bible possessed certain skills of characterization that are far from the natural endowment of the human race. We can analyze the techniques that these skilled storytellers possessed, and when we do, we will begin to understand characterization in stories. Storytellers play such an active role in characterization that it is appropriate to speak of character creation as one of the storyteller's gifts, even when the author uses real-life characters and events.

## Who or What Does the Characterizing?

Where we start our exploration is a little arbitrary, so I will start with the question of who or what does the characterizing in a given part of a story. Of course there is a sense in which the storyteller stands behind the entire story and is the one responsible for the characterizing, but that leaves untouched the specific topics that I am about to discuss. We should accept the fact that the storyteller controls everything as a background postulate or assumption, and then proceed to inquire further into the specific means by which the storyteller orchestrates the process that literary scholars call *character creation.*

First, there are sometimes points during a story when the storyteller steps forward and becomes a presence in the story. At such points we are aware of the storyteller as a character standing before us and drawing our attention to something. Most literary scholars speak of this persona as the *narrator* of the story, but the terms *storyteller* and *author* are equally accurate. The point is that sometimes we are aware of the author as a presence in the story, as palpably before us as the other characters.

To illustrate, we find two examples of characterization by the narrator in a single paragraph in the incident of the substitute bride in the story of Jacob and Laban (Gen. 29:15–20). In addition to giving us objective information about Jacob, Leah, and Rachel, the author steps forward as commentator on the characters when he explains that "Leah's eyes were weak, but Rachel was beautiful in form and appearance" (v. 17). Similarly, after giving us the objective information that Jacob served Laban seven years for Rachel, the narrator adds the commentary that "they seemed to him but a few days because of the love he had for her" (v. 20). The objective data elsewhere in the paragraph constitutes "showing," whereas the author resorts to "telling" when he explains or summarizes something.

In the stories of the Bible, there is very little characterization of this type where the narrator does the characterizing. Overwhelmingly, the storytellers of the Bible show us what characters are like but do not explain anything directly. Perhaps for that reason, we pay special attention when the author does the characterizing.

Second, sometimes a character in a story characterizes another character. This also occurs infrequently, but the moment it happens, we are suddenly aware that someone in the story is directly characterizing another character. For example, the story of Elijah includes a major segment devoted to Elijah's ongoing conflict with the wicked king Ahab (1 Kings 18–22). When Elijah arrives on the scene after Ahab and his wife Jezebel have orchestrated the murder of Naboth, the king greets Elijah with the words, "Have you found me, O my enemy?" (1 Kings 21:20). Through most the story, we *see* the conflict between Elijah and Ahab in action, but for a brief moment Ahab (a character in the story) highlights Elijah's role as his great adversary. It is not as though we cannot infer this from the action, but when Ahab characterizes the prophet as his enemy, the character of Elijah stands out silhouetted in that role with heightened clarity.

Sometimes a character in a biblical story has occasion to characterize himself or herself. We can call this *self-characterization*. Thus when Jacob arrives in Egypt late in his life and stands before King Pharaoh, he expresses in capsule form what his long story in Genesis has displayed: "Few and evil have been the days of the years of my life" (Gen. 47:9). This shorthand self-characterization is a way of saying, "I have lived a difficult and struggle-filled life." As with authorial assertion and characterization by another person in the story, self-characterization packs a particular punch because it stands out from the general field.

What, then, is this general field in which nearly all characterization in biblical narrative is embodied? It is the action or events of a story. In biblical narrative, action is character, and character is action. In contrast to the other three modes of characterization where a *person* summarizes a character, when *action* does the characterizing the task of drawing the right conclusions about a character rests with the reader. We might think that in a sacred book designed to tell us how to live and what to believe the authors would have provided lots of interpretive help to ensure that we reach the right conclusions, but to our surprise the task of getting it right is placed mainly on us.

To summarize, at any moment in a story the characterization is being done by one of four possible agents—the author or narrator, another character in the story, the character himself or herself, and the action. Two conclusions can be drawn from this situation.

First, we can hardly miss the point that characterization in a Bible story is the result of an author's careful design and strategy. The storyteller has made continuous decisions about how to present the characters in a story. A given piece of characterization did not happen automatically; the storyteller chose from among the available methods.

Second, being aware the four potential agents of characterization lets us know how to interact with a given piece of data. When characterization is embodied in action, we understand that we need to be active in drawing the right conclusions about a character. Sometimes there is a certain tentativeness about our conclusions, especially when someone else offers a different view of the matter. By contrast, when one of three characters does the characterizing (the narrator, another character, or the character himself or herself), we usually regard the characterization as "official" and view it as authoritative.

## How the Characterizing Is Done

Having observed the agents of characterizing (as noted in the preceding section), the next plausible thing to note is *the means by which* these four agents or the storyteller behind everything perform their task of characterization. The big division is into the two categories of *direct* assertion or description, and a range of *indirect* means of characterization.

We have already touched upon the most obvious means of direct characterization. It consists of the text itself explicitly attributing a character trait or role to a character. When we read such a statement, we are aware that someone has just summarized an aspect of a character in a story. In turn, these direct statements fall into two categories.

An explicit summary statement about a character is sometimes descriptive or observational, and therefore objective. For example, in the story of the Fall, the narrator tells us flat out that "the serpent was more crafty than any other beast of the field" (Gen. 3:1). To be sure, this is a generalization and judgment call, but the story that follows shows without a doubt that the serpent is clever in manipulating his victim. Satan's craftiness is objectively verifiable and ranks as an observation rather than an interpretation.

The other type of direct characterization is evaluative in nature. Here the summary statement contains an element of assessment, usually falling into the categories of ascribing something favorable or unfavorable to a character. In the story of the separation of Abraham and Lot (Gen. 13), the narrator first gives us a bit of action by telling us that Lot "settled among the cities of the valley and moved his tent as far as Sodom" (v. 12), and then he directly characterizes the residents of Sodom as "wicked, great sinners against the LORD" (v. 13). The latter statement represents direct characterization in an evaluative mode.

But most characterization in the stories of the Bible is indirect rather than direct. Several categories can be discerned here too. First, overwhelmingly in Bible stories, characterization is embodied in the *actions* of a character. When the storyteller simply narrates what a character did, it is up to us to tease out a description of character from that action. In the story of Lot's rescue (Gen. 19), when we read that Lot "lingered" and needed to be dragged out of the city by the angels (v. 16), we are the ones who draw the conclusion that Lot's longstanding laxity in living in a corrupt city has through long habit made him incapable of leaving his sinful lifestyle behind.

A second form of indirect characterization is *dialogue*. When a storyteller puts dialogue before us, we as readers simply overhear what the characters say to each other. Nothing can be more objective and indirect than simply being presented with the words that characters exchange with each other. Faced with this presented material, we need to attribute meaning to the uttered words as part of the process of determining character. In the story of the Egyptian taskmasters and their Jewish slaves (Exod. 1), we overhear the Egyptian king ask the midwives why they have "let the male children live" (v. 18), followed by the midwives' reply that the Hebrew mothers "are vigorous and give birth before the midwife comes to them" (v. 19). It is up to us as readers to see the clever deceptiveness of the midwives and the obtuseness of the king. The characterization is indirect.

Sometimes *tone* can be a means of indirect characterization. Tone refers to the attitude that a storyteller and reader take toward the subject matter. In the incident of Pharaoh and the midwives noted above, the king is in effect mocked by the Jewish author, and the midwives are held up for admiration. These contrasting tones (mockery and admiration) are an indirect means of characterizing Pharaoh and the midwives. In effect we taunt the foreign oppressor and valorize the midwives for their courage and cleverness.

Another indirect means of characterization is the technique known as *foil*. A foil is something that sets off another thing. In stories, a foil is usually a contrast, but it can also be a parallel. In the story of Cain (Gen. 4:1–16), the villainy of the problem child Cain stands out all the more clearly by being contrasted to the virtuous behavior of the model child Abel. The lying of Ananias and Sapphira about how much money they have received from the land they have sold (Acts 5:1–10) is highlighted by the way in which the author inserts the contrasting story of someone who handed over the entire amount that he received for the sale of his land (Acts 4:36–37).

To sum up, here in outline form is an anatomy of the *means by which* an agent of characterization (ultimately the storyteller who orchestrates everything) conducts the task of characterization:

- Direct methods of characterization: (a) assertions or descriptions that make an objective, verifiable statement that summarizes a character or a specific trait, and (b) statements of an evaluative nature that offer an assessment of a character.
- Indirect methods of characterization: (a) actions performed by a character, (b) dialogue, (c) foils that highlight or set off a character or specific traits by being contrasted to their opposites within the story itself, and (d) a tone that calls attention to some feature of a character.

## Determining Character: The Role of Sympathy and Aversion

As we read a story and pay attention to the characters, we intuitively compile a portrait of the characters. The more conscious and deliberate we are about compiling a character profile, the more accurate will be the picture that we compose of each character. We might speak of this process as *determining character*.

A key component in this process is assessing whether a given detail about a character is positive or negative. This, in turn, is tied up with the storyteller's intended message. The stories of the Bible do not exist only for entertainment. They are also comments about life.

How does the author orchestrate the data in such a way as to guide our responses in the desired direction? The answer is so simple as to amaze us: storytellers (including those in the Bible) achieve their persuasive end by controlling our patterns of sympathy and aversion (antipathy) to individual pieces of characterization and ultimately to an entire character. In place of sympathy and aversion we can equally well speak of approval and disapproval of various details about a character.

But isn't there a problem of subjectivity with this? The first answer is that this is simply inherent in the nature of narrative as a literary form. Storytellers achieve their persuasive aim by getting us to feel positively and negatively toward the data of the story. When God entrusted his word to stories, he delegated to us as readers the task of interpreting characters by approving and disapproving of them and their actions.

But we are not by any means left to our own designs in this venture. Storytellers influence our patterns of response to characters. They themselves are a presiding presence in their stories. They use devices of disclosure to guide our responses. Additionally, the stories of the Bible exist in a context of the Bible as a whole, including numerous expository sections that tell us directly how God commands and expects us to live.

## Characterization in the Story of the Exchanged Birthright (Genesis 25:27–34)

The story of Esau's selling of his birthright to Jacob is a brief story that is so concentrated that it will provide good illustrations of the material provided above.

> [27] When the boys grew up, Esau was a skillful hunter, a man of the field, while Jacob was a quiet man, dwelling in tents. [28] Isaac loved Esau because he ate of his game, but Rebekah loved Jacob.
>
> [29] Once when Jacob was cooking stew, Esau came in from the field, and he was exhausted. [30] And Esau said to

Jacob, "Let me eat some of that red stew, for I am exhaust-
ed!" (Therefore his name was called Edom ["Red"].)
[31]Jacob said, "Sell me your birthright now." [32]Esau said,
"I am about to die; of what use is a birthright to me?"
[33]Jacob said, "Swear to me now." So he swore to him and
sold his birthright to Jacob. [34]Then Jacob gave Esau bread
and lentil stew, and he ate and drank and rose and went
his way. Thus Esau despised his birthright.

Since the purpose of my analysis of this story is to illustrate the
various grids and concepts that I have introduced, I will simply
use those categories for my analysis. Who does the characterizing
in this story? The storyteller steps forward as a narrator in three
separate places. In verses 27–28 he offers summary statements of
the characters of Esau and Jacob. The parenthetical statement in
verse 30 is in effect a "time out" in which the narrator says something uncomplimentary about Esau. With the parting shot about
Esau despising his birthright (v. 34), we are strongly conscious
that the storyteller has stepped forward to offer a verdict on what
has just happened.

Except for these three instances where the storyteller stands
before us and does a piece of characterizing, we know Jacob and
Esau by their actions. Whatever portrait emerges from this narration is something that we as readers supply.

By what method is the characterization conducted? Any passage in which the narrator does the characterizing is an example of
the direct method. Thus when we are told that Esau "was a skillful
hunter, a man of the field" (v. 27), that Jacob "was a quiet man,
dwelling in tents" (v. 27), and that Esau "despised his birthright"
(v. 34), we receive these comments as generalizations, or summary statements requiring no further analysis on our part. Are
these summary statements (a) descriptive and objective, or are
they (b) evaluative and interpretive? The statements in verse 27

have qualities of both, while the parting shot (v. 34) is an evaluation of Esau's spiritual state.

When the storyteller resorts to indirect means of characterization (embodying it in action), we need to draw interpretive conclusions. Before I apply this in detail, I want to note the grid of indirect means of characterization that I delineated earlier. I have already asserted that the characters' actions are an indirect means of characterization. Additionally, the whole story of the exchanged birthright is built around a central foil in which Jacob and Esau are portrayed as opposite temperaments. The narrator's early comments in verses 27–28 alert us to this right from the start. We see qualities of both brothers partly because they are set against the other.

Dialogue is an important means of characterization in this brief story. And even tone enters, though we need to resort to information from commentaries to pick up on it. The parenthetical comment about Esau's nickname "Red" is an uncomplimentary jab (ultimately by the Hebrew author at the expense of a surrounding enemy nation known as the Edomites). More to the point, in the original text Esau's speech patterns are rough and unrefined. A legitimate rendition of his request for stew is, "Let me gulp some of that red stuff."

On the basis of these indirect means of characterization, we get an amazingly complete picture of the two principal characters. As we assemble a portrait of Jacob, we come to characterize him as self-seeking, unbrotherly, an opportunist who takes advantage of someone else's need, unscrupulous, manipulative, scheming, and having good business sense (by making Esau swear, Jacob makes sure that the transaction is legally binding). Jacob is the archetypal trickster in this story.

Esau possesses virtually the opposite temperament and therefore displays virtually opposite traits to those of Jacob. Esau lives for the moment and is the slave of his appetites. He cannot delay physical gratification, and he has no capacity for spiritual reality (as represented by the blessing that accompanied the birthright). Esau's emotions are close to the surface (in contrast to Jacob's coolly calculating approach to life), and he is given to overreaction: being hungry becomes exaggerated into the feeling that he is "about to die" (v. 32).

I have analyzed who does the characterizing and by what means. Only when we apply analytic grids like this are we likely to see how complex the data is, and how masterful the storyteller is.

Our final task is to be appropriately introspective and take stock of our responses to the data that our analysis has uncovered. We immediately recoil from Esau. He is our least favorite type of person with whom to deal. Perhaps Jacob requires a little more scrutiny, but upon reflection we conclude that he, too, is offered by the author as an example to avoid imitating in our own lives.

## LEARNING BY DOING

Based on the foregoing theory and application to the story of Jacob and Esau, you are in a good position to try your hand at character analysis. The story of Joseph in his parental home (Gen. 37) is a good text with which to explore characterization according to the methodology proposed above. You can choose either to focus on Joseph only or to apply your analysis to all of the characters. Here is a brief checklist of things to apply:

- Agency: Who or what does the characterizing in a given instance?
- Mode: Does a given piece of data constitute direct characterization or indirect characterization? If the former,

is the statement of commentary a piece of objective description or an evaluative assessment of a character?

- With a given piece of data, do you approve or disapprove of what a character does? Overall, is a given character presented positively or negatively in this story?

¹Jacob lived in the land of his father's sojournings, in the land of Canaan. ²These are the generations of Jacob.

Joseph, being seventeen years old, was pasturing the flock with his brothers. He was a boy with the sons of Bilhah and Zilpah, his father's wives. And Joseph brought a bad report of them to their father. ³Now Israel loved Joseph more than any other of his sons, because he was the son of his old age. And he made him a robe of many colors. ⁴But when his brothers saw that their father loved him more than all his brothers, they hated him and could not speak peacefully to him.

⁵Now Joseph had a dream, and when he told it to his brothers they hated him even more. ⁶He said to them, "Hear this dream that I have dreamed: ⁷Behold, we were binding sheaves in the field, and behold, my sheaf arose and stood upright. And behold, your sheaves gathered around it and bowed down to my sheaf." ⁸His brothers said to him, "Are you indeed to reign over us? Or are you indeed to rule over us?" So they hated him even more for his dreams and for his words.

⁹Then he dreamed another dream and told it to his brothers and said, "Behold, I have dreamed another dream. Behold, the sun, the moon, and eleven stars were bowing

down to me." [10]But when he told it to his father and to his brothers, his father rebuked him and said to him, "What is this dream that you have dreamed? Shall I and your mother and your brothers indeed come to bow ourselves to the ground before you?" [11]And his brothers were jealous of him, but his father kept the saying in mind.

[12]Now his brothers went to pasture their father's flock near Shechem. [13]And Israel said to Joseph, "Are not your brothers pasturing the flock at Shechem? Come, I will send you to them." And he said to him, "Here I am." [14]So he said to him, "Go now, see if it is well with your brothers and with the flock, and bring me word." So he sent him from the Valley of Hebron, and he came to Shechem. [15]And a man found him wandering in the fields. And the man asked him, "What are you seeking?" [16]"I am seeking my brothers," he said. "Tell me, please, where they are pasturing the flock." [17]And the man said, "They have gone away, for I heard them say, 'Let us go to Dothan.'" So Joseph went after his brothers and found them at Dothan.

[18]They saw him from afar, and before he came near to them they conspired against him to kill him. [19]They said to one another, "Here comes this dreamer. [20]Come now, let us kill him and throw him into one of the pits. Then we will say that a fierce animal has devoured him, and we will see what will become of his dreams." [21]But when Reuben heard it, he rescued him out of their hands, saying, "Let us not take his life." [22]And Reuben said to them, "Shed no blood; throw him into this pit here in the wilderness, but do not lay a hand on him"—that he might

rescue him out of their hand to restore him to his father. [23]So when Joseph came to his brothers, they stripped him of his robe, the robe of many colors that he wore. [24]And they took him and threw him into a pit. The pit was empty; there was no water in it.

[25]Then they sat down to eat. And looking up they saw a caravan of Ishmaelites coming from Gilead, with their camels bearing gum, balm, and myrrh, on their way to carry it down to Egypt. [26]Then Judah said to his brothers, "What profit is it if we kill our brother and conceal his blood? [27]Come, let us sell him to the Ishmaelites, and let not our hand be upon him, for he is our brother, our own flesh." And his brothers listened to him. [28]Then Midianite traders passed by. And they drew Joseph up and lifted him out of the pit, and sold him to the Ishmaelites for twenty shekels of silver. They took Joseph to Egypt.

[29]When Reuben returned to the pit and saw that Joseph was not in the pit, he tore his clothes [30]and returned to his brothers and said, "The boy is gone, and I, where shall I go?" [31]Then they took Joseph's robe and slaughtered a goat and dipped the robe in the blood. [32]And they sent the robe of many colors and brought it to their father and said, "This we have found; please identify whether it is your son's robe or not." [33]And he identified it and said, "It is my son's robe. A fierce animal has devoured him. Joseph is without doubt torn to pieces." [34]Then Jacob tore his garments and put sackcloth on his loins and mourned for his son many days. [35]All his sons and all his daughters rose up to comfort him, but he refused to be comforted and said, "No, I shall go down to Sheol

> to my son, mourning." Thus his father wept for him.
> [36]Meanwhile the Midianites had sold him in Egypt to
> Potiphar, an officer of Pharaoh, the captain of the guard.

## Final Thoughts on Characterization as Done by Authors

The primary takeaway value of this chapter is to increase your awareness that characterization in Bible stories does not just happen. It is the product of numerous strategy decisions on the part of the storyteller. It stands to reason that with experienced storytellers, many of these decisions are intuitive rather than consciously thought out, but it remains the case that there are always multiple ways to tell a story. The story as it stands is just one of those ways.

Storytellers decide whether to use the narrative voice or a statement by another character in the story, or whether to let action embody the characterization. They decide whether to use dialogue in some part of the story, or narrate the material by recounting action. They decide whether to include a certain piece of data, or to withhold it.

If characterization in a Bible story is the product of such decisions, as readers we need to be analytic about the composition that is put before us. If the storytellers of the Bible are sophisticated in the ways I have delineated, as readers we need to raise the bar in terms of our awareness and our willingness to engage in analysis of the techniques that are embedded in the text and lie behind it.

An obvious application of these matters is that a story as it stands is different from how it would have been if the author had made other choices. One decision is of particular importance. The central character in a story is known as the *protagonist*, based on the Greek word "first struggler" or "first combatant." Forces arrayed against this first struggler go by the name *antagonist*. As readers we need to "go with the flow" in regard to the storyteller's decision. We need to view ourselves as the traveling companion of the central character, going through the story from that character's point of view.

This requires us to avoid some common practices in evangelical circles. One is to skew a story toward good characters even when they are not the protagonists of the story. As part of that bias, some readers turn virtually every story in the Bible into an optimistic "good news" story. In the story of Cain (Gen. 4:1–16), Abel is the model character, but he is not the protagonist. He is a functional character who provides the occasion for the central action, and once he has played that role, he drops out of the story. In this story, God does extend mercy to Cain at some points, but overall the story is a story of judgment.

Even more pervasive is the practice of claiming that God is the hero (and by implication the protagonist) of every story in the Bible. God is the ultimate being in every story of Bible. He is a named character in many (but not) all Bible stories. But only rarely is God the protagonist (the first struggler) in the stories of the Bible.

This chapter has put forward several important types of characters (always the product of an author's choices, we need to remind ourselves). They include protagonist, antagonist, sympathetic character, and unsympathetic character. Several other categories are useful to have in our repertoire as we make sense of biblical stories. There is a lot to be gained by dividing characters into the categories of *major character* and *minor character*. They are major and minor on the basis of how much space they get in a story, not in terms of their being good or bad.

A category of minor characters is known as *functional characters*. They appear in a story to perform a function required by the plot. The author could have given them more space, but their role is to perform a function for the plot and nothing more. A *blocking character* is a character who stands in the way of other people's happiness or purposes. In the Gospels, the scribes and Pharisees regularly feature in the stories as blocking characters to Jesus. In the story of the ten plagues, the Egyptian king Pharaoh is a blocking character for Moses and the Israelites.

## Summary

Characterization in stories is more complex than we usually realize. There is always more than one way to tell a story. The author either consciously or intuitively made many decisions in regard to the presentation of characters in a story. As readers, we can develop the skill of picking up on a storyteller's decisions. It is not the claim of this chapter that we always need to apply all of the considerations to every story of the Bible. The point is only that we will do a better job of getting to know characters in a Bible story in the manner that the next chapter will develop if we are aware of the material covered in this chapter. Additionally, we can begin to practice the suggestions of the present chapter intuitively as they become familiar to us. We rather quickly come to realize that (1) someone or something is doing the characterizing in a Bible story, (2) by either direct or indirect means, and that (3) we need to respond positively or negatively to the characters and their traits and actions.

# 4

# Characterization in Bible Stories (Part 2)

## *What Readers Need to Do*

The preceding chapter provided an anatomy of ways in which storytellers manage the portrayal of characters in their stories. The types of analysis proposed in that chapter provide useful ways of seeing what is actually going on in the stories of the Bible. The various decisions that authors make impose a range of interpretive tasks on us. If an author decides to embody characterization in dialogue, we need to be active in a way that is not required when he uses the narrative voice to tell us that "Joseph was handsome" (Gen. 39:6).

Despite the benefits of mastering the information and analytic tools of the preceding chapter, however, I need to clarify that the information covered in the preceding chapter is not what primarily yields the portraits of biblical characters. Analysis of how storytellers manage their feats of characterization is not by itself the thing that makes up a biblical character. This chapter covers the elements that actually comprise a character in a Bible story.

## What Makes Up the Substance of a Character in a Bible Story?

Regardless of who does the characterizing and by what means, the elements that actually make up a character in a story are the following things:

- *Physical actions.* This subject made an appearance in the preceding chapter also (as a means of indirect characterization), and the fact that it now shows up on the list of ingredients that make up a character is an index to its importance. We know what characters in a story are like by what they do. It is as simple as that. When Jacob takes advantage of his brother's hunger and impulsiveness, he shows himself to be a scheming and selfish person.

- *Mental actions or thoughts,* including motivations for what characters do. What biblical characters think is as much a part of their make-up as what they do. We immediately need to acknowledge how rarely the storytellers in the Bible tell us what a character is thinking. Sometimes, of course, they do tell us. When Jacob was bracing himself for his reunion with Esau after twenty years of separation, he divided his family members and animals into two camps. Why? The author takes us inside his thought process: Jacob thought, "If Esau comes to the one camp and attacks it, then the camp that is left will escape" (Gen. 32:8). To make thought processes explicit like this is extremely rare in the stories of the Bible (in contrast to the modern novel, where a large share of the action is interior and psychological). This does not mean that there is no psychology in the stories of the Bible; it only means that for the most part we need to *infer* the thoughts of a character (including motivations for action).

- *Words.* This is admittedly a broad category, but we need to have it on our grid. What a character does and thinks is important, but so is what a character says. There are two main types of characterization based on words. One consists of the *content* of what a character says. When Jesus tells the paralytic, "My son, your sins are forgiven" (Mark 2:5), we understand that Jesus is the one who forgives sins. The second aspect of verbal actions is the *style* of the words—the type of language and its arrangement. *How* a character speaks tells us much about that character. Jesus' famous beatitudes (Matt. 5:3–12) by their very style characterize Jesus as a poet and master of rhetorical (or oratorical) speech.

- *Feelings or emotions.* This category belongs with the previous three and completes a cluster: physical actions, mental actions, verbal actions, and feelings. As with thoughts, we largely need to infer a biblical character's emotions from the situation in a story. When the youthful Jacob kisses the pretty Rachel at the town well "and wept aloud" (Gen. 29:11), we know him at that moment by his implied feelings. An example of a character's feelings made explicit occurs when we read that Jesus was "moved with pity" during his encounter with a leper (Mark 1:41).

- *Traits and abilities.* Naming the traits of a character is at the heart of determining character in Bible stories. Only occasionally does a storyteller name the trait of a character, in the manner of the narrator's telling us that "Esau was a skillful hunter" (Gen. 25:27). Almost always we infer a character's abilities from the other things that appear in this list of elements of characterization. We need to note, however, that the goal of character analysis is to assemble a portrait, or profile, of a character, and this usually takes the form of a list of the character's traits and abilities.

- *Relationships and roles.* This dimension is often overlooked in analysis of characterization in stories. Yet it is crucial. We know Jacob and Esau partly by their roles as brothers. We know Abraham partly by his relationship to God, partly by his domestic roles (husband, father), and partly by his role as sojourner in Egypt and wanderer in Canaan.

- *Responses to events or people.* In stories, as in life, one of the clearest glimpses that we get into a person is the immediate response to an event. The immediate response is intuitive and springs from the soul of a person. When Esau comes home hungry after a hunting excursion, his immediate response is to place his appetite higher in priority that every other value, while Jacob's immediate response is to scheme to take advantage of his brother. As with a camera click, the identity of both brothers stands highlighted simply by their responses to an immediate situation.

- *Archetypal character types.* The key element with an archetype is that it recurs throughout literature and life. One category of archetypes is character types. Examples are hero, villain, traveler, tyrant, benevolent king or parent, virtuous wife, and martyr. The moment we correctly name the archetype to which a character belongs, we have established an important part of that person's identity.

## Description and Interpretation

Analysis of characterization falls into two distinct categories. One is observation, or description. It asserts something that is objectively true and verifiable. Often it covers the literal facts surrounding a character. To call Cain a murderer is a descriptive statement.

An interpretive statement about a character is more subjective. It builds on the literal or observational data. It involves attributing meaning or significance to the literal facts. It might involve making an assessment about whether a given detail is positive or negative, good or bad, sympathetic or unsympathetic.

We engage in continuous small or localized acts of interpretation as we assemble a portrait of characters in a Bible story. In the story of Elijah's duel with the prophets of Baal on Mount Carmel (1 Kings 18:20–40), the text merely narrates what Elijah did. We then build upon this factual data and attribute the qualities of courage and faith in God to Elijah. In the story of Peter's denial of Jesus, to say that Peter betrayed Jesus is to make a descriptive statement, but we move to an interpretive level when we infer that Peter was fearful and cowardly.

Analysis of a character in a Bible story requires both description and interpretation. We need to get the facts surrounding a character straight. But to remain at this level is to miss the deeper significance of the stories of the Bible. Even at the level of storytelling, we are not content to remain at an observational level.

The distinction between description/observation and interpretation is mainly something of which we need to be aware. It does not yield a methodology to the same degree that the grid of elements of a character does. If we are aware of the categories of description and interpretation, we can strike a balance between description and interpretation when dealing with a biblical character.

## Characterization in the Call of Gideon (Judges 6:11–18, 25–27, 36–40)

Gideon is a developing character in the three chapters of Judges (6–8) devoted to his story. In these chapters we read about the making of a hero, which implies that Gideon is far from heroic at the beginning of the story. The following account of his call (abbreviated here in the interests of keeping the material manageable) allows us to apply the methodology that has been presented above.

> [11]Now the angel of the LORD came and sat under the terebinth at Ophrah, which belonged to Joash the Abiezrite, while his son Gideon was beating out wheat in the winepress to hide it from the Midianites. [12]And the angel of the LORD appeared to him and said to him, "The LORD is with you, O mighty man of valor." [13]And Gideon said to him, "Please, sir, if the LORD is with us, why then has all this happened to us? And where are all his wonderful deeds that our fathers recounted to us, saying, 'Did not the LORD bring us up from Egypt?' But now the LORD has forsaken us and given us into the hand of Midian." [14]And the LORD turned to him and said, "Go in this might of yours and save Israel from the hand of Midian; do not I send you?" [15]And he said to him, "Please, LORD, how can I save Israel? Behold, my clan is the weakest in Manasseh, and I am the least in my father's house." [16]And the LORD said to him, "But I will be with you, and you shall strike the Midianites as one man." [17]And he said to him, "If now I have found favor in your eyes, then show me a sign that it is you who speak with me. [18]Please do not depart from here until I come to you and bring out my present and set it before you." And he said, "I will stay till you return." . . .
>
> [25]That night the LORD said to him, "Take your father's bull, and the second bull seven years old, and pull down the altar of Baal that your father has, and cut down the Asherah that is beside it [26]and build an altar to the LORD your God on the top of the stronghold here, with stones

laid in due order. Then take the second bull and offer it as a burnt offering with the wood of the Asherah that you shall cut down." ²⁷So Gideon took ten men of his servants and did as the LORD had told him. But because he was too afraid of his family and the men of the town to do it by day, he did it by night. . . .

³⁶Then Gideon said to God, "If you will save Israel by my hand, as you have said, ³⁷behold, I am laying a fleece of wool on the threshing floor. If there is dew on the fleece alone, and it is dry on all the ground, then I shall know that you will save Israel by my hand, as you have said." ³⁸And it was so. When he rose early next morning and squeezed the fleece, he wrung enough dew from the fleece to fill a bowl with water. ³⁹Then Gideon said to God, "Let not your anger burn against me; let me speak just once more. Please let me test just once more with the fleece. Please let it be dry on the fleece only, and on all the ground let there be dew." ⁴⁰And God did so that night; and it was dry on the fleece only, and on all the ground there was dew.

My purpose in looking at this passage is to illustrate the grid of things that make up a character in a story, as follows:

- *Physical actions.* In sequence, Gideon does the following things: beats out wheat in a concealed place; converses with an angel of God; hesitates to accept his call to be a leader; asks the angel for confirming signs; tears down a pagan altar in his home town by night because he is afraid to do it by day. This list is descriptive in nature. But we need to do something *with* these actions as we move toward a character profile for Gideon. Here is a corresponding list of interpretive statements based on the premise that Gideon's identity consists of what he does. Gideon is (1) repeatedly timid and defeatist in his outlook; (2) resistant to all suggestions that he can be a heroic leader; (3) obedient to what the angel of God commands him to do, and thereby capable of heroic action; (4) persistent in resisting the call to leadership.

- *Mental actions.* Gideon is repeatedly shown to be fearful and defeatist in his outlook. He is quick with his mind in resisting the call to leadership, and correspondingly slow to accept that call. As we infer Gideon's process of thinking, we come to think of him as a reluctant hero and someone who does not want to be a hero.

- *Words.* The story of Gideon is a hero story, even though Gideon gradually *becomes* a hero instead of starting there. In keeping with this, Gideon's language and speech patterns show him to be a leader. We can say of Gideon already here at the start of the story that he speaks well and even eloquently. His words to the angel are reverent and respectful.

- *Feelings or emotions.* It is easy to infer that Gideon feels inferior and timid in the face of what he is called to do.

- *Traits and abilities.* Gideon's primary trait in this phase of his story is his reluctance to become a leader, perhaps based on an inferiority complex. Counterbalancing this trait is the repeated evidence that he has the ability to become a heroic leader. Here at the outset of the story we are presented with a paradox: Gideon has the ability to become a leader, but he does not want to become one.

- *Relationships and roles.* We see Gideon relating to quite a range of persons: his family, his community, the angel of God, and his servants. We do not view Gideon as a solitary figure but a person firmly entrenched in a community and attuned to the supernatural world.

- *Responses to events or people.* In relation to the occupying Midianites and his fellow Israelites, Gideon does what he is called to do but in a timid manner. His immediate response to the appearance of the angel is to be fearful, respectful, complaining, obedient, and persistent. His response to the call to leadership is to delay in accepting the role.
- *Archetypes.* In this passage Gideon is the archetypal reluctant hero.

## LEARNING BY DOING

The story of the separation of Abraham and Lot as narrated in Genesis 13 is a good test case for applying the grid of elements that make up a literary character. The grid has already been presented twice and does not need to be repeated here. Since Abraham and Lot get approximately equal space, each should be analyzed separately. While an in-class lecture on characterization in a story or a critical essay on it might be arranged according to the grid, in actual analysis the right procedure is to work our way through the story sequentially, verse by verse. We might think of this as doing spadework preliminary to presenting a profile of a character. For every verse or piece of data, the right question to ask is, What do I know about this character on the basis of this detail?

> [2]Now Abram was very rich in livestock, in silver, and in gold. [3]And he journeyed on from the Negeb as far as Bethel to the place where his tent had been at the beginning, between Bethel and Ai, [4]to the place where he had made an altar at the first. And there Abram called upon the name of the LORD. [5]And Lot, who went with Abram,

also had flocks and herds and tents, ⁶so that the land could not support both of them dwelling together; for their possessions were so great that they could not dwell together, ⁷and there was strife between the herdsmen of Abram's livestock and the herdsmen of Lot's livestock. At that time the Canaanites and the Perizzites were dwelling in the land.

⁸Then Abram said to Lot, "Let there be no strife between you and me, and between your herdsmen and my herdsmen, for we are kinsmen. ⁹Is not the whole land before you? Separate yourself from me. If you take the left hand, then I will go to the right, or if you take the right hand, then I will go to the left."

¹⁰And Lot lifted up his eyes and saw that the Jordan Valley was well watered everywhere like the garden of the LORD, like the land of Egypt, in the direction of Zoar. (This was before the LORD destroyed Sodom and Gomorrah.) ¹¹So Lot chose for himself all the Jordan Valley, and Lot journeyed east. Thus they separated from each other.

¹²Abram settled in the land of Canaan, while Lot settled among the cities of the valley and moved his tent as far as Sodom. ¹³Now the men of Sodom were wicked, great sinners against the LORD.

¹⁴The LORD said to Abram, after Lot had separated from him, "Lift up your eyes and look from the place where you are, northward and southward and eastward and westward, ¹⁵for all the land that you see I will give to you and to your offspring forever. ¹⁶I will make your offspring as

> the dust of the earth, so that if one can count the dust of the earth, your offspring also can be counted. [17]Arise, walk through the length and the breadth of the land, for I will give it to you." [18]So Abram moved his tent and came and settled by the oaks of Mamre, which are at Hebron, and there he built an altar to the LORD.

## Final Thoughts on Characterization in Bible Stories

The first thing to do in regard to the characters in a story is to assemble the cast of characters. That may seem simple minded, but it yields big results. After all, how does a printed version of a play begin? With a list of the cast of characters, sometimes accompanied by a brief identifying role or trait for some of the characters. We can profitably do the same thing as we begin our analysis of characterization in a story.

Having assembled the cast of characters, it is a good idea to divide them into the two categories of primary characters and secondary characters, based on the amount of space they get in the story. There are other ways of naming these two categories, including major and minor characters, and protagonist and antagonist(s).

The nearly inevitable pattern in stories is for storytellers to put characters in situations that test them. This becomes a useful analytic paradigm, as we take note of what characters reveal about themselves during the process of being tested. Every choice that a character in a story makes is an implied test for that character.

I have stressed the need for readers of Bible stories to engage in both descriptive and interpretive analysis. The starting point for good character analysis is a keen eye for the obvious. We should not disparage this level of interaction. We need to get the facts straight. The second skill required in character analysis is massaging the literal facts surrounding a character into an interpretive portrait of that character.

But one more step remains. We need to ask what the storyteller is saying about life with his or her characters. A good story strikes a balance among the three ingredients of a story (setting, character, plot). In the actual experience of the story, all three are probably equally important. Nonetheless, if we ask which of those three is the primary vehicle in which the storyteller embodies his message about life, I think that the answer is the characters.

## Summary

The goal of character analysis in stories is for us to get to know the characters as fully as possible, and then to decide what the author intends us to learn about life and God on the basis of these characters. If the grid of ingredients ever starts to become burdensome, the foregoing sentence can serve as a shortcut that will enable us to do a creditable job with the characters in Bible stories. Nonetheless, the grid of ingredients is easy to apply and ensures that our approach will be systematic and thorough.

# 5

# Plot Structure and Unity

## The Beginning, Middle, and Ending of a Story

Plot is one of three elements that make up every story. Action is a good synonym for plot. But further things characterize the action that makes up a plot, and they are the subject of this chapter.

The first thing to grasp is that a plot is *a sequence* of events. It is not a random collection of unrelated events but a chain of related events in which one event produces the next one, and so forth. The most frequently cited authority on plot is the Greek thinker Aristotle, and his way of describing the sequence of events that make up a plot was to say that a plot has a beginning, a middle, and an end. That may seem simplistic, but it is actually profound.

Aristotle's formula draws attention to two important features of a plot. The first is that a plot is a coherent whole. Every individual incident is part of a single action. In fact, Aristotle said regarding the individual units that "we must see that they are relevant to the action." Secondly, Aristotle's formula of beginning-middle-end asserts that the incidents unfold sequentially according to a cause-effect logic. The middle is the chain of events by which we move from the initial situation to the final one.

With the above information serving as a foundation, this chapter will cover three aspects of plot. They all have to do with the big, overriding aspects of a plot. The next chapter will provide close-ups within the large framework that is covered in this chapter.

## The Sequential Structure of a Plot

As already implied, a plot is made up of a chain of related events. There are multiple words that we can use to name these units: scenes (based on the model of drama), episodes, events, or even acts (as in drama—act 1, act 2, etc.).

The primary obligation that the sequential nature of plot places on us can be called *identifying the action*. What this means is that as readers we need to divide the plot into its successive units and name them accurately. Both of these deserve a bit of unpacking.

Dividing a plot sequence into its constituent parts requires analysis, first of all. The goal is to produce an outline of the story. During the spadework phase of this analysis, it is very useful to draw horizontal lines to divide the sequence into easily seen units. Photocopying the passage or printing it from the Internet is freeing, as opposed to drawing lines in a Bible.

In this process of dividing the plot into its parts, there is usually not just one right way to outline the action. For one thing, we usually have an option between dividing the story into its smallest possible units or going for a somewhat streamlined version (big effects as opposed to exhaustive and minute units). The group or occasion for which we are preparing a lesson might be an influence. We need to avoid overloading an audience with too many details. On the other hand, in private analysis there is definitely a place for the fine-toothed-comb approach. We see certain things more clearly if we look at them close up and in detail.

In addition to dividing the plot into its successive building blocks, we need to name those parts. The first requirement here is that our labels be accurate. But a second layer also emerges, namely, the need to name the individual units in such a way as to keep the central action in view. The name by which this is usually called is the whole-part relationship. Of course when we start our spadework we may not yet have a clear view of what the unifying action is. But once we have formulated our preferred version of the unifying action, we can go back and bring our labels for individual parts into line with the unifying core of the plot.

## Overriding Unifying Action

Outlining a plot according to its successive units is one version of the unity of a story. We can think of this as the sequential unity of a plot, showing how the story unfolds in linear fashion. But a plot also possesses a spatial unity by which we see the story all at once—not as a linear structure but a single entity. This is the single unifying action of a plot.

Here are four examples of how the core plot of a story can be formulated as a single action in which we see the whole story as in a photograph:

- The story of the fall in Genesis 3 is a story of crime and punishment. The sequential structure of the plot is directly related to that and falls into three parts: what led up to the crime, the committing of the crime, and the consequences of the crime.
- The big unifying action in the story of Gideon (Judg. 6–8) is Gideon's deliverance of his nation from the oppression of the Midianites.

- The story of Daniel and his three friends in the court of King Nebuchadnezzar (Dan. 1) is unified by the motif of testing. We observe the circumstances that led up to the test, the process of testing, and the results of the test.
- The core action in the story of Jesus and the Samaritan woman at the well (John 4:1–42) is Jesus' quest to bring the woman to saving faith in him.

Some stories introduce a complexity into the situation by being stories with multiple plots. This happens relatively infrequently, but the story of Abraham (Gen. 12–25) incorporates three overall storylines: the quest of Abraham for land and a son; God's progressive revelation of his covenant to Abraham; the ongoing conflict within Abraham between faith and expediency. All three unify the story as a whole.

## Plot Conflict

There is one more aspect of plot unity, and its importance cannot be overstated. It is in the very nature of a plot to be constructed around one or more conflicts. This is simply inherent in the concept of plot. We have never adequately accounted for the plot in a given story until we have determined the plot conflicts that are woven into the plot.

Stories do not announce what the plot conflicts are. We need to determine them. This takes time and mental energy. We need to expend that time and mental energy with every story that we aspire to master.

There is one more dimension to this. Stories are built around plot conflicts that are resolved at the end of the story. The paradigm into which all plots fall is that of *plot conflict moving to resolution*. It is as important to analyze and state the resolution of the plot conflicts as it is to identify the conflicts. If we do not perform this additional analysis, we leave the plot conflicts dangling in mid-air.

It is also useful to note the possible types of plot conflicts. The grid is as follows:

- character conflict (characters in conflict with each other)
- conflict with one's environment (either nature or society)
- conflict with supernatural beings
- inner conflict (characters in conflict with themselves)

There is one more grid of conflicts that yields dividends when we apply it to stories, based on the type of conflict (not the agent of conflict, as in the preceding grid). Plot conflicts can be (1) physical in nature, (2) psychological (either mental or emotional), or (3) moral or spiritual.

## Plot in the Story of Paul and Silas in Philippi (Acts 16:16–40)

The goal of the following analysis of the story of what happened to Paul and Silas during their missionary visit to the city of Philippi is to illustrate the features of plot that have been delineated above. Those features are three in number: plot sequence, unifying action, and plot conflicts.

> [16]As we were going to the place of prayer, we were met by a slave girl who had a spirit of divination and brought her owners much gain by fortune-telling. [17]She followed Paul and us, crying out, "These men are servants of the Most High God, who proclaim to you the way of salvation." [18]And this she kept doing for many days. Paul, having become greatly annoyed, turned and said to the spirit, "I command you in the name of Jesus Christ to come out of her." And it came out that very hour.

[19]But when her owners saw that their hope of gain was gone, they seized Paul and Silas and dragged them into the marketplace before the rulers. [20]And when they had brought them to the magistrates, they said, "These men are Jews, and they are disturbing our city. [21]They advocate customs that are not lawful for us as Romans to accept or practice." [22]The crowd joined in attacking them, and the magistrates tore the garments off them and gave orders to beat them with rods. [23]And when they had inflicted many blows upon them, they threw them into prison, ordering the jailer to keep them safely. [24]Having received this order, he put them into the inner prison and fastened their feet in the stocks.

[25]About midnight Paul and Silas were praying and singing hymns to God, and the prisoners were listening to them, [26]and suddenly there was a great earthquake, so that the foundations of the prison were shaken. And immediately all the doors were opened, and everyone's bonds were unfastened. [27]When the jailer woke and saw that the prison doors were open, he drew his sword and was about to kill himself, supposing that the prisoners had escaped. [28]But Paul cried with a loud voice, "Do not harm yourself, for we are all here." [29]And the jailer called for lights and rushed in, and trembling with fear he fell down before Paul and Silas. [30]Then he brought them out and said, "Sirs, what must I do to be saved?" [31]And they said, "Believe in the Lord Jesus, and you will be saved, you and your household." [32]And they spoke the word of the Lord to him and to all who were in his house. [33]And he took them the same hour of the night and washed their wounds; and he was baptized at once, he and all his family. [34]Then he brought them up into his house

and set food before them. And he rejoiced along with his entire household that he had believed in God.

$^{35}$ But when it was day, the magistrates sent the police, saying, "Let those men go." $^{36}$ And the jailer reported these words to Paul, saying, "The magistrates have sent to let you go. Therefore come out now and go in peace." $^{37}$ But Paul said to them, "They have beaten us publicly, uncondemned, men who are Roman citizens, and have thrown us into prison; and do they now throw us out secretly? No! Let them come themselves and take us out." $^{38}$ The police reported these words to the magistrates, and they were afraid when they heard that they were Roman citizens. $^{39}$ So they came and apologized to them. And they took them out and asked them to leave the city. $^{40}$ So they went out of the prison and visited Lydia. And when they had seen the brothers, they encouraged them and departed.

As we apply the three main considerations to a given story, we should not feel a burden to hit a supposed target of one right way to formulate the issues. Usually we are in a position of choosing from a menu of good options. Below is one good way (but not the only good way) to view plot in the story of Paul and Silas in prison.

- *Unifying action.* The story we are looking at falls into the category of prison narrative. The core action is the imprisonment and release of Paul and Silas.
- *Sequential structure.* The process of outlining the phases of action can profitably be thought of as *identifying the action.* Two preliminary considerations are that (1) we always need to label the parts in such a way as to keep the focus on our formulation of unifying action, and (2) in

most situations we need to strike a compromise between unduly brief outlines and overly minute or detailed outlines. Here is an outline that meets those criteria:

   o   verses 16–18: prelude to the imprisonment

   o   verses 19–24: attack on Paul and Silas ending in imprisonment

   o   verses 25–26: miraculous breaking of the prison bonds

   o   verses 27–34: interaction with the jailor ending in the salvation of him and his household

   o   verses 35–39: negotiations with the city officials over the imprisonment

   o   verse 40: release from prison

- *Plot conflicts.* Paul and Silas in conflict with the following: the annoying slave girl (vv. 16–18); the spirit of divination in the slave girl (v. 18); the slave girl's owners (v. 19); the Jewish leaders and city magistrates (vv. 20–24); the oppressive bondage of the prison (v. 24); the fear and threatened suicide of the jailor (vv. 27–30); the city magistrates (vv. 35–38). At various moments a given plot conflict in this story is resolved by the casting out of the slave girl's spirit (v. 18), by God's miraculous intervention (v. 26), by the saving message of the gospel (vv. 31–34), by the apology of the city officials after they learn about the credentials of Paul and Silas (vv. 38–39), and by the official release from prison (v. 40).

It is obvious from this plenitude of material that there is no scarcity of analysis that can be done with plot structure and unity.

## LEARNING BY DOING

The threefold grid of sequential structure, unifying action, and plot conflict has been fully explained above. It is now your chance to try your hand at analysis with the story of Abraham's offering of Isaac in Genesis 22:1–19.

> [1]After these things God tested Abraham and said to him, "Abraham!" And he said, "Here I am." [2]He said, "Take your son, your only son Isaac, whom you love, and go to the land of Moriah, and offer him there as a burnt offering on one of the mountains of which I shall tell you." [3]So Abraham rose early in the morning, saddled his donkey, and took two of his young men with him, and his son Isaac. And he cut the wood for the burnt offering and arose and went to the place of which God had told him. [4]On the third day Abraham lifted up his eyes and saw the place from afar. [5]Then Abraham said to his young men, "Stay here with the donkey; I and the boy will go over there and worship and come again to you." [6]And Abraham took the wood of the burnt offering and laid it on Isaac his son. And he took in his hand the fire and the knife. So they went both of them together. [7]And Isaac said to his father Abraham, "My father!" And he said, "Here I am, my son." He said, "Behold, the fire and the wood, but where is the lamb for a burnt offering?" [8]Abraham said, "God will provide for himself the lamb for a burnt offering, my son." So they went both of them together.
>
> [9]When they came to the place of which God had told him, Abraham built the altar there and laid the wood in order and bound Isaac his son and laid him on the altar, on top

of the wood. [10]Then Abraham reached out his hand and took the knife to slaughter his son. [11]But the angel of the LORD called to him from heaven and said, "Abraham, Abraham!" And he said, "Here I am." [12]He said, "Do not lay your hand on the boy or do anything to him, for now I know that you fear God, seeing you have not withheld your son, your only son, from me." [13]And Abraham lifted up his eyes and looked, and behold, behind him was a ram, caught in a thicket by his horns. And Abraham went and took the ram and offered it up as a burnt offering instead of his son. [14]So Abraham called the name of that place, "The LORD will provide"; as it is said to this day, "On the mount of the LORD it shall be provided."

[15]And the angel of the LORD called to Abraham a second time from heaven [16]and said, "By myself I have sworn, declares the LORD, because you have done this and have not withheld your son, your only son, [17]I will surely bless you, and I will surely multiply your offspring as the stars of heaven and as the sand that is on the seashore. And your offspring shall possess the gate of his enemies, [18]and in your offspring shall all the nations of the earth be blessed, because you have obeyed my voice." [19]So Abraham returned to his young men, and they arose and went together to Beersheba. And Abraham lived at Beersheba.

## Final Thoughts on Plot Structure and Unity

The track record of study Bibles and commentaries on the subjects of plot structure and unity is not as good as it should be. There is a general scarcity of published material on these matters (and also on setting and characterization). In fact, here is a brief list of pitfalls to avoid when you read published material on Bible stories:

- An overly detailed outline of the successive units of the story. If you or your audience cannot keep the scheme in mind, it is too detailed to be useful.
- An overly abstract and theological labeling of the plot and its units. A storyteller does not have a topic to present and a thesis to develop. He has a story to tell. Additionally, a story does not have a unifying topic but a unifying *action*.
- Outlines that might attach accurate labels to a given unit but that do not keep the central unifying action in view.
- Overly tidy or schematic outlines that do not do justice to the specificity of the text. Outlines that make heavy use of alliteration are especially suspect.

It needs to be said again that these sins of commission are accompanied by sins of omission (saying nothing about plot sequence and unifying action and plot conflicts).

If published sources do not provide the needed information or provide misleading information, what can you do? You can practice what this book imparts. You do not need published material. You need the right methodology with which to interact with Bible stories.

This guided study is a how-to-do-it book. By now you have convinced yourself that you can conduct literary analysis of biblical narratives. That is all you need in order to perform good literary analysis of Bible stories. Anyone can divide a story into its successive units and identify plot conflicts and formulate an accurate statement of the unifying action of a story. All it takes is being convinced that these are the right things to do with a story.

# Plot Devices

## *How Storytellers Tell Their Story with Beauty and Skill*

The preceding chapter covered the big, overriding aspects of a plot, namely, its structure and unity. Those features are relevant to the plot as a whole. The focus of this chapter is the more localized places in a story where smaller aspects of plot become operative. For lack of a better term, we can call these *devices* of plot. They are pervasive in any carefully constructed story, and we need to be able to interact with them in the right ways when they make their appearance as we are reading along.

### Devices at the Start of a Story

Some of the plot elements that make up this chapter can more naturally be called *conventions* of plot—strategies that storytellers from time immemorial have used when composing a story. The devices that meet us at the beginning of a story fall into this category of plot conventions.

The opening phase of every plot is known as *exposition*. Exposition can be thought of as background material. We should think of this material as conveying to us the "givens" of the story—the things that will be taken for granted in the story that follows. The data that we receive in the exposition can be viewed as supplying two essential things.

First, considered in light of the plot that is about to unfold, the exposition supplies the ingredients that *enables* the action of the story. The things that the storyteller decides to put before us at the outset are the things that make the plot possible. Once that information has been assembled, the plot conflict(s) can be introduced into the story and the plot can begin. Often this shift from background to action is very specific and obvious. Literary critics speak of the second stage of the plot as the *inciting moment,* or *inciting agent*. It is the mini-explosion that is dropped into the accumulated pool of background information.

If we look at the exposition from the reader's point of view instead of the author's, we can view it as telling us what *we* need to know in order to understand the story that is about to unfold. Viewed in this way, the exposition does not enable the plot but instead enables the reader to understand the story.

What are the actual ingredients of an exposition? There is no set formula, but here are the things that typically appear in the exposition of a story: introduction of at least some of the cast of characters; often an indication of who the protagonist is, and at least some of the antagonists; preliminary information about the setting of the story; an introduction of the ingredients that might eventuate in a plot conflict. Additionally, in keeping with the concept that was introduced in the chapter on setting that when we read a story we enter a whole narrative world, the exposition is our entry into that world. Often we catch hints of the main aspects of that world.

There is yet another way to view the exposition. An essential of any good story is that it transports us from our time and place to another time and place. Most storytellers use certain formulas to signal that the reader is now making a break with ordinary reality and transitioning to a world that will exist in their imagination. Here are five story openings from the Bible to illustrate this quality of letting us know that a story is now beginning: "now there was a famine in the land" (Gen. 12:10); "once when Jacob was cooking stew" (Gen. 25:29); "now the angel of the LORD came" (Judg. 6:11); "one day Elisha went on to Shunem" (2 Kings 4:8); "on that day, when evening had come" (Mark 4:35). "Now," "once," "one day," "on that day": all of these terms are formulaic, signaling that a story is now beginning.

What responsibility do these rituals of beginning impose on the reader of a Bible story? Primarily we need to pay closer attention to the opening sentences or verses of a story than we typically do. The storyteller is playing by the rules of the game. He is establishing the ingredients that will enable the plot, and he is informing us of what we need to know in order to follow the story. We need to be alert to the rituals of opening that have been carefully assembled for us.

## Plot Devices in the Middle of a Story

Once the inciting moment has propelled a plot into the phase known by literary critics as *rising action,* various plot devices begin to appear. These devices are so recurrent that we might view them as the building blocks of a plot. The most important of these devices are the following (listed in random order):

### *Foreshadowing*

Foreshadowing occurs when something in a story makes us aware of something that will occur later in the story. Two things are important about a moment of foreshadowing. The first is that once the foreshadowing has been established, we look for its fulfillment. The second is that when the foreshadowed event actually happens, we remember the prediction. In effect we experience the event or situation twice.

Foreshadowing takes two forms—direct and subtle. In direct or explicit foreshadowing, the storyteller or a character in the story gives us information about something that will happen later. A prophecy or prediction can function as foreshadowing. Thus in the story of Gideon's defeat of the Midianites, when the men of Penuel refuse to give his army food, Gideon claims that when he returns after defeating the Midianites he will tear down the tower of Penuel (Judg. 8:9). This prediction and threat are a foreshadowing of what actually happens later in the story (v. 17).

Usually, however, foreshadowing is subtle and indirect. We as readers need to recognize an implied foreshadowing (and of course we may not recognize it on a first reading when we are ignorant of the later fulfillment). For example, because we know that Samson's Nazirite vow requires him not to cut his hair as a pre-condition of his strength, when he tells Delilah that he will become weak if his hair is cut (Judg. 16:17), we experience it as a foreshadowing of what later happens to him.

### Suspense

Suspense is a moment in a story where we are led to wonder what will happen next, or how an action will turn out. In the story of Joseph, he suffers so many misfortunes that through most of the story we are left wondering (held in suspense) about how the opening dreams of Joseph's being over his family can possibly be fulfilled. Again, in the story of the stolen blessing, when Jacob enters the tent of Isaac in disguise (Gen. 27:18), we are gripped with suspense over whether or not Isaac will recognize that he is Jacob instead of Esau.

## Testing

The archetypal plot motif of testing is more pervasive in stories than many people realize. The test motif enters a story in an obvious manner when the plot turns upon the motif of testing. The story of Abraham's offering of Isaac is announced right at the outset as a story in which "God tested Abraham" (Gen. 22:1). Joseph's chastity is tested when Potiphar's wife attempts to seduce him (Gen. 39:6–12). What is not so evident is that the most customary situation into which a storyteller places the leading characters in a story is situations that test them. This implied testing will become evident to us if pay attention to how often characters in stories are shown making a choice. Any situation that requires a character to make a choice is an implicit test of what the character is like.

## Poetic Justice

This is a somewhat unfortunate phrase that we nonetheless cannot do without. Poetic justice consists of virtue rewarded and vice punished. Whenever we are strongly aware that virtue has been rewarded and vice punished, we can speak of poetic justice as a plot device. Many stories end with poetic justice, and when they do, the appearance of such justice functions as a tipping of the hand by the storyteller to show what we are meant to approve and disapprove in the characters and events of the story. However, poetic justice can happen along the way and not only at the end of a story.

## Surprise and Reversal of Expectation

Most stories spring surprises on us along the way. The human race loves the plot motif of surprise, and we can agree that life itself has a tendency to include surprises. Sometimes the surprise in a story is so acute as to constitute a reversal of expectation and a change of direction in the flow of the plot.

## The Shape of the Plot in the Middle

The exact ingredients that make up the stages of a plot depend on how long or short the story is. Aristotle said that a plot has a beginning, a middle, and an end. The beginning and end are pretty well set (see above and below), but what about the middle?

For fully developed stories (all the way from the story of Joseph to a Shakespearean play to a modern novel), the following scheme devised by modern literary critics and known as the well-made plot is remarkably constant: exposition → inciting moment or inciting agent → rising action → turning point → further complication → climax → denouement (tying up of loose ends). The turning point should not be confused with climax; the climax comes late in a story, while the turning point occurs in the middle and is the point from which (at least in retrospect) we can see how the plot will be resolved, even though we do not yet know the journey by which we will reach that resolution.

With the longer stories in the Bible, this paradigm is worth its weight in gold because it imposes an order on the plot and enables us to see its unity. Here is how the well-made plot works for the story of Joseph:

1. *Exposition*: Joseph in his family environment
2. *Inciting moment*: selling Joseph into Egypt
3. *Rising action*: Joseph's early fortunes in Egypt, ending in imprisonment
4. *Turning point*: the journey of Joseph's brothers to Egypt
5. *Further complication*: Joseph's testing of his brothers
6. *Climax*: Joseph's disclosure of his identity to his brothers

7. *Denouement*: Jacob's moving to Egypt and the death of Joseph

There is no claim here that this is the only way to organize the plot of the Joseph story. It is only to say that the framework of the well-made plot yields big dividends, and additionally it is an index to the fact that a story is carefully crafted (any story that falls easily into the scheme of the well-made plot can be trusted to be a well-crafted story).

With more briefly narrated stories, we need to operate with a simpler scheme. For brief stories, a simple linear scheme is more workable. Here we can chart growing intensification of action leading to a climax or resolution, but without a discernible rising action, turning point, and further complication. In the story of the exchanged birthright (Gen. 25:29–34), for example, the intrigue that Jacob pulls off at the expense of Esau becomes more and more intense as it unfolds, and the climax comes as we watch Esau eat bread and lentil stew. Then the intensity subsides as we observe Esau leave the scene, having "despised his birthright" (v. 34).

## Forms of Irony

It might seem excessive to give irony its own section in this chapter, but it is entirely appropriate. Irony is one of the chief forms of the order that storytellers impose on their materials. Irony is based on discrepancy between two things, and there are three forms of irony that have attracted storytellers. The first two occur only intermittently and would not elicit special treatment, but the third type of irony is so pervasive that we might well conclude that storytellers cannot ply their trade without it.

*Verbal irony* occurs when someone makes a statement that is actually the opposite of what is the intended meaning. The reader or listener is expected to pick up on this discrepancy; without such recognition, the whole enterprise falls flat and we stand a good chance of not understanding the story at that point.

There is an element of pretense with verbal irony, as the person who utters the statement knows very well that the statement is untrue. In fact, we need a definition of verbal irony that includes statements in which a speaker says what everyone knows to be false. For example, Aaron fashioned his famous golden calf "with a graving tool" (Exod. 32:4), but when Moses called him to account, he claimed that he "threw [gold] into the fire, and out came this calf" (v. 24). Aaron himself knew that this was not true. Verbal irony occurs only rarely in Bible stories, but when it appears, it packs a particular punch.

*Irony of situation* occurs when a situation is so contrary to what is expected or appropriate that we are jolted by it. Often the incongruity is so extreme that we experience it as a bit of wry humor. For example, the prophet Jonah was a prophet by profession, and additionally his name meant "dove" (with associations of peace). He is the son of Amittai, and that name means "truth." Jonah's actions are totally incongruous with that: he attempts to run away from God instead of speaking a prophetic word to Nineveh, and the only thing that his fellow sailors know about him is that "he was fleeing from the presence of the LORD, because he had told them" (Jonah 1:10).

Irony of situation occurs often in the Bible, but the "big one" is *dramatic irony*. Both within and beyond the Bible, storytellers are absolutely addicted to dramatic irony. It occurs when readers know something of which one or more characters in the story are ignorant. This discrepancy of levels of knowledge is ironic. It is a rare story of any length that does *not* have dramatic irony in it. To stick with Jonah for a moment longer, we know that no one can hide from God (see Ps. 139:7–12 for the definitive statement on this truth). Yet Jonah apparently thinks that he can manage this

ironic impossibility. The irony becomes intensified when we hear
Jonah tell the sailors that he serves "the God . . . who made the sea"
(1:9), while at the very moment Jonah is attempting to flee from
God on the sea that God made! We receive that statement as brim-
ming with irony, which (however) escapes the awareness of Jonah.

## Conventions of Closing

Most plots move toward a decisive event near the end that bears
the name of climax. There may have been additional climactic
moments earlier in the story, but at some level a major event
also occurs near the end. In the story of Daniel in the lions' den
(Dan. 6), the climax comes with the casting of Daniel's accusers
into the lions' den in punishment for their attempted execution
of Daniel (v. 24). Peter's third denial of Jesus, accompanied by
the crowing of the rooster, is the climax of the story of Peter's
temptation and betrayal (Luke 22:54–62). While a plot climax
is a ritual of storytelling, we should avoid forcing a given story
into that mold if there is no obvious candidate for being considered a climax.

Stories do not simply end. They are rounded off with a note
of closure and finality. Part of this closure is known as the *denouement* of a plot. This refers to the tying up of loose ends—bringing
the reader up to date on the final outcome of the issues that have
made up the preceding story. The menu of options from which a
storyteller chooses include the following:

- a brief recapitulation of the main action
- a summary of the immediate results of the action that has
  been narrated
- a summary of the long-term effects of the action
- an account of the fortunes that later befall one or more
  characters in the preceding story

- some echo or reminder of what happened earlier, or of the issue that began the plot
- narrating the physical departure of one or more characters to a new place, thereby drawing a boundary around the preceding action

Earlier we noted formulas that signaled the beginning of a story. But closings in Bible stories are also governed by stock formulas, or conventions. Here are examples of formulas that signal a plot ending:

- Change of location and therefore of an action: "So Abram went up from Egypt, he and his wife and all that he had, and Lot with him, into the Negeb" (Gen. 13:1).
- Filling in the information about what happened to a character after the preceding action: "Meanwhile the Midianites had sold [Joseph] in Egypt to Potiphar, an officer of Pharaoh, the captain of the guard" (Gen. 37:36).
- Summary of preceding action and a look into the future: "So Midian was subdued before the people of Israel, and they raised their heads no more. And the land had rest forty years in the days of Gideon" (Judg. 8:28).
- Change of scene and action: "And immediately [Jesus] got into the boat with his disciples and went to the district of Dalmanutha" (Mark 8:10).
- Summary of the effect of the preceding action on the people who lived through it: "And great fear came upon the whole church and upon all who heard of these things" (Acts 5:11).

Unless we are thinking in terms of the rituals of narrative closing, we are likely to be dull-minded and not see how carefully storytellers impart a sense of closure to their stories.

## Plot Devices in the Story of Ehud's Assassination of Eglon (Judges 3:15–26)

Earlier chapters in this book included grids that we should systematically apply as we work our way through stories—grids that list the elements in characterization, for example, or the formula scene of _____ or _____ scene when tracking setting in a story. The items discussed above *can* be used in that way (for example, we might work our way through a story looking for irony), but that is not their most natural use. Instead we need to allow these plot devices to be in our awareness as we work our way through a story, recognizing them when they appear. For purposes of illustrating these elements, I will work my way through the story of Ehud's assassination of Eglon unit by unit, naming the plot devices that appear in which unit. I have named the elements but have not explained how they function in this particular story; I encourage my readers to do that additional act of interpretation. For ease of reference, I have allowed each verse to begin with the left margin of the page.

15: Then the people of Israel cried out to the LORD, and the LORD raised up for them a deliverer, Ehud, the son of Gera, the Benjaminite, a left-handed man. The people of Israel sent tribute by him to Eglon the king of Moab.

    *Plot Element:* Exposition, or background information. The author concisely packs in an amazing quantity of information whose deeper meanings we need to tease out.

16: And Ehud made for himself a sword with two edges, a cubit [18 inches] in length, and he bound it on his right thigh under his clothes.

    *Plot Element:* Foreshadowing; dramatic irony (inasmuch as Ehud's left-handedness leads him to carry his weapon on the unexpected right side, where it escapes detection; it is in effect a disguise).

17: And he presented the tribute to Eglon king of Moab. Now Eglon was a very fat man.
   *Plot Element:* Foreshadowing.

18: And when Ehud had finished presenting the tribute, he sent away the people who carried the tribute.
   *Plot Element:* Foreshadowing (subtle, to be sure, but the point is that Ehud is an opportunist who manages to be alone with his adversary Eglon, leading us to suspect that he will do something clever).

19: But he himself turned back at the idols near Gilgal and said, "I have a secret message for you, O king." And he commanded, "Silence." And all his attendants went out from his presence.
   *Plot Element:* Foreshadowing; suspense; dramatic irony (we know something that Eglon does not); surprise (the characters in the story, and we with them, had no reason to expect that Ehud would return to Eglon's palace; it is something out of the routine in a story that has followed the path of the routine up to this point).

20: And Ehud came to him as he was sitting alone in his cool roof chamber. And Ehud said, "I have a message from God for you." And he arose from his seat.
   *Plot Element:* More dramatic irony and suspense.

21: And Ehud reached with his left hand, took the sword from his right thigh, and thrust it into his belly.
   *Plot Element:* The first climax in this story; poetic justice (there are many subtle hints that Eglon is an oppressive

exploiter of the Israelites and also a worshiper of pagan idols); irony of situation (in the sense that we do not expect a "secret message" and "a message from God" to consist of a sword in the belly); surprise and reversal.

22: And the hilt also went in after the blade, and the fat closed over the blade, for he did not pull the sword out of his belly; and the dung came out.
  *Plot Element:* Poetic justice (the author and his nation would have relished this account of the foreign oppressor who got his comeuppance).

23: Then Ehud went out into the porch and closed the doors of the roof chamber behind him and locked them.
  *Plot Element:* Further complication after the first climax of the story.

24: When he had gone, the servants came, and when they saw that the doors of the roof chamber were locked, they thought, "Surely he is relieving himself in the closet of the cool chamber."
  *Plot Element:* Dramatic irony.

25: And they waited till they were embarrassed. But when he still did not open the doors of the roof chamber, they took the key and opened them, and there lay their lord dead on the floor.
  *Plot Element:* Final climax of the story; surprise (for the king's attendants, who thought that the king was going to the toilet and found out that he was lying dead on the floor).

26: Ehud escaped while they delayed, and he passed beyond the idols and escaped to Seirah.
  *Plot Element:* Denouement, with some conventional rituals of closing.

It was noted above that an important plot device is the testing of characters. This applies globally to the story of Ehud's assassination of Eglon. Ehud is above all a clever and resourceful hero. In every verse, his cleverness and resourcefulness are tested and displayed.

## LEARNING BY DOING

It is time to try your hand at discovering plot devices in a specimen Bible story. There is no doubt that we have had a lot of balls in the air in this chapter, but the devices that have been introduced are familiar to anyone who feels at home with literary narratives. Indeed, we have done no more than identify the storytelling techniques that both storytellers and readers have liked most in stories from time immemorial. For purposes of this exercise, I have selected the story of the stolen blessing (Gen. 27:1–30). This represents a shortened version of the story, which has the interaction between Isaac and Esau as an "add on." Do not overlook that once Jacob enters the tent his ability to maintain his disguise and pull of the deception is tested.

> [1]When Isaac was old and his eyes were dim so that he could not see, he called Esau his older son and said to him, "My son"; and he answered, "Here I am." [2]He said, "Behold, I am old; I do not know the day of my death. [3]Now then, take your weapons, your quiver and your bow, and go out to the field and hunt game for me, [4]and prepare for me delicious food, such as I love, and bring it to me so that I may eat, that my soul may bless you before I die."
>
> [5]Now Rebekah was listening when Isaac spoke to his son Esau. So when Esau went to the field to hunt for game

and bring it, [6]Rebekah said to her son Jacob, "I heard your father speak to your brother Esau, [7]'Bring me game and prepare for me delicious food, that I may eat it and bless you before the LORD before I die.' [8]Now therefore, my son, obey my voice as I command you. [9]Go to the flock and bring me two good young goats, so that I may prepare from them delicious food for your father, such as he loves. [10]And you shall bring it to your father to eat, so that he may bless you before he dies." [11]But Jacob said to Rebekah his mother, "Behold, my brother Esau is a hairy man, and I am a smooth man. [12]Perhaps my father will feel me, and I shall seem to be mocking him and bring a curse upon myself and not a blessing." [13]His mother said to him, "Let your curse be on me, my son; only obey my voice, and go, bring them to me."

[14]So he went and took them and brought them to his mother, and his mother prepared delicious food, such as his father loved. [15]Then Rebekah took the best garments of Esau her older son, which were with her in the house, and put them on Jacob her younger son. [16]And the skins of the young goats she put on his hands and on the smooth part of his neck. [17]And she put the delicious food and the bread, which she had prepared, into the hand of her son Jacob.

[18]So he went in to his father and said, "My father." And he said, "Here I am. Who are you, my son?" [19]Jacob said to his father, "I am Esau your firstborn. I have done as you told me; now sit up and eat of my game, that your soul may bless me." [20]But Isaac said to his son, "How is it that you have found it so quickly, my son?" He answered, "Because

the LORD your God granted me success." [21]Then Isaac said to Jacob, "Please come near, that I may feel you, my son, to know whether you are really my son Esau or not." [22]So Jacob went near to Isaac his father, who felt him and said, "The voice is Jacob's voice, but the hands are the hands of Esau." [23]And he did not recognize him, because his hands were hairy like his brother Esau's hands. So he blessed him. [24]He said, "Are you really my son Esau?" He answered, "I am." [25]Then he said, "Bring it near to me, that I may eat of my son's game and bless you." So he brought it near to him, and he ate; and he brought him wine, and he drank.

[26]Then his father Isaac said to him, "Come near and kiss me, my son." [27]So he came near and kissed him. And Isaac smelled the smell of his garments and blessed him and said,

"See, the smell of my son
        is as the smell of a field that the LORD has blessed!
[28]May God give you of the dew of heaven
        and of the fatness of the earth
        and plenty of grain and wine.
[29]Let peoples serve you,
        and nations bow down to you.
Be lord over your brothers,
        and may your mother's sons bow down to you.
Cursed be everyone who curses you,
        and blessed be everyone who blesses you!"

[30]As soon as Isaac had finished blessing Jacob, when Jacob had scarcely gone out from the presence of Isaac his father, Esau his brother came in from his hunting.

## Final Thoughts on Plot Devices

What is the function of plot devices in a story? First, they add to the craftsmanship that we can admire in a story. Obviously all story, including the stories in the Bible, are the product of a storyteller's skill. The storytellers of the Bible had mastered the skill of storytelling. They know how to manipulate the resources of their chosen form of narrative. The stories of the Bible only *appear* to be artless.

Additionally, the impact of a story depends on the presence of plot devices. This is simply an assumption that we need to make. A literary scholar who wrote a book on the dynamics of narrative claimed that the function of narrative form (another name for plot devices) is "to silhouette the material with the desired degree of clarity." Let's take the story of Ehud the resourceful southpaw as a test case. The main issues in this story—the evil represented by a pagan and exploitive foreign king, the courage and resourcefulness of Ehud, the heroism of Ehud, the administration of justice—all these stand out clearly because of the presence of features like testing and dramatic irony and climax.

But there is even more at stake than simply the effectiveness of the story. English author T. S. Eliot took the matter a step further when he wrote that "it is the function of all art to give us some perception of an order in life, by imposing an order upon it." In other words, it is not only the story that is clarified and made effective by plot devices. Life is also clarified by them. Plot devices like dramatic irony and poetic justice constitute the "order" that Eliot identifies—an order imposed on the materials of life.

The result is that a carefully composed story is more than a recording of events from life. It is an expression of life that is given meaning. Sometimes literary scholars draw an analogy to a painting that we hang on the wall. The painting represents life framed and selected and molded. As just one small extension of that, the opening and closing rituals mentioned in this chapter make a story like a picture that is framed. Bible stories represent life organized and framed so we can see it clearly. The result is that stories often give us a heightened experience of life.

There are more plot devices than the ones covered in the body of this chapter. Here is a brief selective list:

- *Scene of discovery*, or *recognition* scene, as when Esau enters Isaac's tent and both of them suddenly realize that Jacob has deceived his father and stolen the blessing.
- *Deception scene.*
- *Intrigue* (secretive, behind-the-scenes scheming).
- *Reversal of action.* There are actually two types of plot reversal. In one, the tables are suddenly turned and the action takes on an opposite or distinctly different direction. Thus the Israelite army is totally intimidated by the Philistine giant Goliath, until David's killing of him in battle changes the situation. But reversal can also be an action that is the opposite of what a character intended. Isaac blessed a son, thinking that it was his preferred son Esau, when actually it was Jacob.
- *Reunion scene.*
- *Adventure.*

All of these are elements of plot that we need to identify when a story puts them before us.

Finally, literary scholars sometimes produce a *taxonomy of types of plots*. These can help us organize our experiences of stories in the Bible. Some stories highlight the changing circumstances of the protagonist and can appropriately be viewed as *change of fortune stories*. In other stories the focus falls on character; such stories can be called *stories of character*. To literary scholars, a U-shaped story in which events descend into potential tragedy and then rise to a happy ending is called a *comic plot*. On the other hand, a *tragic plot* narrates the fall of a character from prosperity to calamity.

## Summary

If we ask, Are the plot devices covered in this chapter important and essential to our analysis of the Bible story? the answer is yes. They are the components of a story. They help to explain the effects that a Bible story produces on us, but beyond that, they are the things that silhouette the important patterns in a story. We have not fully experienced a story without interacting with the plot devices. Furthermore, these devices often give us a heightened perception of life (as in the formula of T. S. Eliot quoted above).

# 7

# Hero Stories

## A Neglected but Fruitful Narrative Genre

his will be a short and concentrated chapter. The central concept is simple, but it is too important to fold into the categories covered in the preceding chapter devoted to plot devices. One of the greatest weaknesses of traditional biblical scholarship is its failure to cultivate an awareness of the genre of hero stories. It is an easy gap to fill, and it is the purpose of this chapter to do so.

## Toward a Definition of Hero Story

A hero story is a story built around a central protagonist who is held up for admiration. There are many additional nuances that need to be added, but the central concept is simple. The main focus of a hero story is the character and exploits of the hero.

How important are hero stories? The answer is that most stories are hero stories. The genre of narrative is thus almost synonymous with the subgenre of hero story. Furthermore, the impulse behind hero stories is synonymous with the impulse behind literature itself—to give expression and shape to our own experiences. The fact that we hear so little about the genre of hero story is evidence of a great abdication. In not being initiated into the genre of hero story, the Bible reading public has been deprived of one of its greatest resources.

If a hero story is defined by the focus of the action on a central hero, the important further question is what a hero is. Here are the defining traits of a literary hero:

- A hero is the protagonist or leading character in a story. We can legitimately use the adjective "heroic" for an exemplary minor character, but such a character is not the hero of the story. A literary hero is the protagonist of a story.

- The hero is representative. Heroes embody the experiences, conflicts, and struggles of the culture or group producing them. Heroes might be so universal as to represent virtually the entire human race, or they might represent a specific group or subculture.

- A hero not only represents the *experiences* of a culture or group but also embodies the *values* of that group. A hero story thus codifies what an author and audience believe and try to practice. We can thus call the hero an *exemplary* figure—someone who serves as an example to follow and emulate in our own lives.

- As an extension of that, it is a ground rule of hero stories that these stories not only present a certain kind of character but also answer the implied question of *what constitutes heroic action*. Hero stories answer the question of what constitutes the good life and the proper way of living.

- In view of this, a hero is a generally idealized character who embodies an ideal. Heroes and heroines need not be wholly idealized (good and admirable), but they are largely so. If they are not, we should not call them heroes and heroines.
- A hero possesses qualities that capture people's imaginations. One of the functions of heroes is to serve as an inspiration, so we can legitimately ask in what ways we find a hero or heroine inspiring.

It is important to realize that real life does not produce a hero as just defined. Real life gives us the *materials* from which heroes can be constructed. A literary hero is always the product of an author's selectivity and molding. Some real-life materials are omitted during the process of authorial selectivity. We can say that a storyteller *distills* some aspect of a character and presents that to us in heightened form.

## The Methodology for Analyzing a Hero Story

The methodology for analyzing a hero story comes straight from the definition that has been presented above. In fact, we can turn the definition of a literary hero into a series of questions to ask and answer from the text, as follows:

1. What experiences, conflicts, and struggles does the hero enact?
2. As seen in the hero's character and actions, what represents the right way to live? What values does the story offer for approval? What constitutes heroic action?
3. Knowing that a hero is usually a combination of positive and negative traits (but always with the former the dominant element), what character traits does the story

encourage us to emulate and what negative traits are offered as errors to avoid?

4. What traits of the hero capture the popular imagination? What do we find inspiring about a hero or heroine?

These questions are good ones to have in our awareness as we move through a hero story. They can also guide us when we stand back from a hero story as a whole and organize our final thoughts on it.

## The Story of Daniel in the Lions' Den as a Hero Story (Daniel 6:1–24)

For purposes of this book, I needed to choose a suitably short narrative. I feel led to say, however, that the greatest hero stories of the Bible are on the long side—the stories of Joseph, Gideon, Daniel, Ruth, and Esther, for example. Of course we realize that the story of Jesus as narrated in the Gospels is the ultimate hero story.

When compared to these substantial hero stories, the two that I selected for this chapter seem just a little undersized—great, but giving us a glimpse of heroism rather than a full portrait of it as found in longer stories. For purposes of illustrating the definition and methodology that I presented above, the story of Daniel in the lions' den will serve admirably (Dan. 6:1–24).

> [1]It pleased Darius to set over the kingdom 120 satraps, to be throughout the whole kingdom; [2]and over them three high officials, of whom Daniel was one, to whom these satraps should give account, so that the king might suffer no loss. [3]Then this Daniel became distinguished above all the other high officials and satraps, because an excellent spirit was in him. And the king planned to set him over the whole kingdom. [4]Then the high officials and

the satraps sought to find a ground for complaint against Daniel with regard to the kingdom, but they could find no ground for complaint or any fault, because he was faithful, and no error or fault was found in him. ⁵Then these men said, "We shall not find any ground for complaint against this Daniel unless we find it in connection with the law of his God."

⁶Then these high officials and satraps came by agreement to the king and said to him, "O King Darius, live forever! ⁷All the high officials of the kingdom, the prefects and the satraps, the counselors and the governors are agreed that the king should establish an ordinance and enforce an injunction, that whoever makes petition to any god or man for thirty days, except to you, O king, shall be cast into the den of lions. ⁸Now, O king, establish the injunction and sign the document, so that it cannot be changed, according to the law of the Medes and the Persians, which cannot be revoked." ⁹Therefore King Darius signed the document and injunction.

¹⁰When Daniel knew that the document had been signed, he went to his house where he had windows in his upper chamber open toward Jerusalem. He got down on his knees three times a day and prayed and gave thanks before his God, as he had done previously. ¹¹Then these men came by agreement and found Daniel making petition and plea before his God. ¹²Then they came near and said before the king, concerning the injunction, "O king! Did you not sign an injunction, that anyone who makes petition to any god or man within thirty days except to you, O king, shall be cast into the den of lions?" The king answered and said, "The thing stands fast, according to the law of the Medes and Persians, which cannot

be revoked." [13]Then they answered and said before the king, "Daniel, who is one of the exiles from Judah, pays no attention to you, O king, or the injunction you have signed, but makes his petition three times a day."

[14]Then the king, when he heard these words, was much distressed and set his mind to deliver Daniel. And he labored till the sun went down to rescue him. [15]Then these men came by agreement to the king and said to the king, "Know, O king, that it is a law of the Medes and Persians that no injunction or ordinance that the king establishes can be changed."

[16]Then the king commanded, and Daniel was brought and cast into the den of lions. The king declared to Daniel, "May your God, whom you serve continually, deliver you!" [17]And a stone was brought and laid on the mouth of the den, and the king sealed it with his own signet and with the signet of his lords, that nothing might be changed concerning Daniel. [18]Then the king went to his palace and spent the night fasting; no diversions were brought to him, and sleep fled from him.

[19]Then, at break of day, the king arose and went in haste to the den of lions. [20]As he came near to the den where Daniel was, he cried out in a tone of anguish. The king declared to Daniel, "O Daniel, servant of the living God, has your God, whom you serve continually, been able to deliver you from the lions?" [21]Then Daniel said to the king, "O king, live forever! [22]My God sent his angel and shut the lions' mouths, and they have not harmed me, because I was found blameless before him; and also before you, O king, I have done no harm." [23]Then the king was exceedingly glad, and commanded that Daniel be taken up out of the den. So Daniel was taken up out of

the den, and no kind of harm was found on him, because he had trusted in his God. <sup>24</sup>And the king commanded, and those men who had maliciously accused Daniel were brought and cast into the den of lions—they, their children, and their wives. And before they reached the bottom of the den, the lions overpowered them and broke all their bones in pieces.

What conflicts and struggles of the culture are producing the story? Daniel enjoyed the favor of three different Persian kings, but in the final analysis he belonged to a captive nation that was always being opposed and persecuted by their surrounding pagan culture. By extension, virtually any religious person can see his or her situation embodied in Daniel's predicament.

What constitutes heroic action? Heroic action consists of being loyal to God, being courageous in worshiping God despite opposition and even persecution, and trusting God in the worst imaginable extremities of life (even the threat of death).

What character traits does the story affirm or offer for approval? The portrait of Daniel is wholly idealized, so we cannot name any failings (even though that is an ingredient in most hero stories). The traits of Daniel offered for approval and emulation are his courage, devotion to God, integrity, and practice of prayer.

What traits of the hero capture the popular imagination? The children's hymn "Dare to Be a Daniel" provides good answers. The superlative degree of Daniel's courage and religious devotion are what most capture our imagination. Daniel is so exemplary that even a pagan king admires him, and his opponents know that the only possible way to trip Daniel up is through his religious devotion.

## LEARNING BY DOING

The Old Testament stories of Ruth and Esther are among the high points of storytelling in the Bible, and they are both hero stories par excellence. The following passage is an excerpt from the story of Esther. At the beginning of the story, Esther is a beautiful but weak-willed young woman, who lives a life of compromise as she wins the king's heart. At the moment of crisis, she becomes a hero of the faith. The following excerpt is taken from that phase of the story. The backdrop for the action narrated below is that when Esther's uncle Mordecai put pressure on Esther to intervene for her nation when Haman orchestrated a threat to the Jews, Esther initially refused to get involved. That is where the following action kicks in (Esther 4:12–17; 5:1–5; 7:1–6; 8:3–8).

> [12]And they told Mordecai what Esther had said. [13]Then Mordecai told them to reply to Esther, "Do not think to yourself that in the king's palace you will escape any more than all the other Jews. [14]For if you keep silent at this time, relief and deliverance will rise for the Jews from another place, but you and your father's house will perish. And who knows whether you have not come to the kingdom for such a time as this?" [15]Then Esther told them to reply to Mordecai, [16]"Go, gather all the Jews to be found in Susa, and hold a fast on my behalf, and do not eat or drink for three days, night or day. I and my young women will also fast as you do. Then I will go to the king, though it is against the law, and if I perish, I perish." [17]Mordecai then went away and did everything as Esther had ordered him.
>
> [5:1]On the third day Esther put on her royal robes and stood in the inner court of the king's palace, in front of the king's

quarters, while the king was sitting on his royal throne inside the throne room opposite the entrance to the palace. ²And when the king saw Queen Esther standing in the court, she won favor in his sight, and he held out to Esther the golden scepter that was in his hand. Then Esther approached and touched the tip of the scepter. ³And the king said to her, "What is it, Queen Esther? What is your request? It shall be given you, even to the half of my kingdom." ⁴And Esther said, "If it please the king, let the king and Haman come today to a feast that I have prepared for the king." ⁵Then the king said, "Bring Haman quickly, so that we may do as Esther has asked." So the king and Haman came to the feast that Esther had prepared....

⁷:¹So the king and Haman went in to feast with Queen Esther. ²And on the second day, as they were drinking wine after the feast, the king again said to Esther, "What is your wish, Queen Esther? It shall be granted you. And what is your request? Even to the half of my kingdom, it shall be fulfilled." ³Then Queen Esther answered, "If I have found favor in your sight, O king, and if it please the king, let my life be granted me for my wish, and my people for my request. ⁴For we have been sold, I and my people, to be destroyed, to be killed, and to be annihilated. If we had been sold merely as slaves, men and women, I would have been silent, for our affliction is not to be compared with the loss to the king." ⁵Then King Ahasuerus said to Queen Esther, "Who is he, and where is he, who has dared to do this?" ⁶And Esther said, "A foe and enemy! This wicked Haman!" Then Haman was terrified before the king and the queen....

8:3 Then Esther spoke again to the king. She fell at his feet and wept and pleaded with him to avert the evil plan of Haman the Agagite and the plot that he had devised against the Jews. 4When the king held out the golden scepter to Esther, 5Esther rose and stood before the king. And she said, "If it please the king, and if I have found favor in his sight, and if the thing seems right before the king, and I am pleasing in his eyes, let an order be written to revoke the letters devised by Haman the Agagite, the son of Hammedatha, which he wrote to destroy the Jews who are in all the provinces of the king. 6For how can I bear to see the calamity that is coming to my people? Or how can I bear to see the destruction of my kindred?" 7Then King Ahasuerus said to Queen Esther and to Mordecai the Jew, "Behold, I have given Esther the house of Haman, and they have hanged him on the gallows, because he intended to lay hands on the Jews. 8But you may write as you please with regard to the Jews, in the name of the king, and seal it with the king's ring, for an edict written in the name of the king and sealed with the king's ring cannot be revoked."

The grid by which to organize your thoughts about this story as a hero story is simple: (1) As representative of her religious group, how does the story of Esther enact the conflicts and struggles of believers living in exile? (2) What pattern does Esther's life offer for emulation, and what constitutes heroic action according to this story? (3) What is admirable about Esther's character and actions? (4) How does Esther capture the popular imagination of all who read her story?

## Final Thoughts on Hero Stories

The importance of the following principle cannot be overstated: *a hero story is a generic story first of all, and a hero story after that.* All that we have covered about narrative in general in the preceding chapters of this book needs to be applied hero stories. The considerations of hero story presented in this chapter are an additional layer of description and interpretation that we need to apply to hero stories. Accordingly, the material presented in this chapter is not a substitute for ordinary narrative analysis.

The most plausible place to bring the considerations of hero story into play is as a retrospective look back over the story after ordinary narrative analysis is complete. The grid of hero story considerations is extremely useful as a putting-it-all-together venture at the end of an analysis of a hero story. Part of that usefulness is extracting the themes and edification of a hero story—its takeaway value.

But that is not the only use that we should make of the considerations of hero story covered in this chapter. At many points in our journey through a hero story our awareness of the definition of a hero story can shed light on a localized detail in the story. In particular, we have many occasions to ask, "What is heroic about _____?" as we work our way through a hero story.

A final useful tip is to be aware that heroes and heroines fall into recognizable categories and archetypes. Naming these helps to pinpoint and summarize a hero or heroine. For example, Abraham is a religious and domestic hero. Esther is a national heroine. Gideon and Ehud are military heroes. Literary scholars also use the formula "the hero as _____" (the hero as worshiper, as warrior, as person on a quest), or "the _____ as hero" (the priest as hero, the shepherd as hero, the mother as hero).

## Summary

Considerations of the genre hero story are not a substitute for ordinary narrative analysis, but we have never fully assimilated a hero story if we do not also apply the grid of considerations for a hero story. It is also impossible to overstate the importance of having the concept of hero story in our repertoire of literary skills. The most numerous category of stories is hero stories.

# 8

# From Story to Meaning

## How to Find Significance in a Narrative Text

Up to this point, this guide to biblical narrative has focused on how to interact with Bible stories as stories. We can appropriately think of this as dealing with literary form— the "how" of biblical narrative. It is the prerequisite to everything else we might do with a Bible story. We cannot extract the "what" without first interacting with the "how." The first item on our agenda as readers of Bible stories needs to be *reliving the story as fully as possible*. Unless we do that, we will be cutting against the grain.

Additionally, when we immerse ourselves in a Bible story as a story, we have already assimilated its edification in *indirect or latent form*. If we relive the story of Daniel in the lions' den or Ruth and Boaz falling in love and marrying, we have absorbed part of the religious meaning of those stories.

Nonetheless, we have never adequately assimilated the truth of a Bible story if we do not move beyond its literary form and explicitly address the moral and religious ideas in the story. Many people do not know how to extract the religious meaning of a text if that text is a narrative. This chapter is designed to leave you convinced that you can move from story to meaning with confidence.

## Seeing Life Accurately

The ideas embodied in a Bible story are an important part of the truth that these stories communicate, but we need to start by challenging the prevalent assumption that ideas are the only form of truth that exists. The particular niche of literature is *truthfulness to human experience and life.* We can think of this as *representational truth*—the truth that comes from seeing life pictured or represented accurately—as distinct from *ideational truth.*

This book began with a chapter titled "The Subject of Every Story." The concept asserted and illustrated in that chapter is that literature embodies human experience and presents it so concretely that we relive that experience in our imagination. We can think of ourselves as observing life as we absorb a Bible story. As we stare at reality in this way, we come to see it clearly and accurately. This is knowledge in the form of right seeing, and it is a form of truth that we need. If we do not see something clearly, we do not possess the truth about it.

Representational truth is not the subject of this chapter. That was the subject of the opening chapter. Nonetheless, we need to keep that concept on our radar screen as we think about the truthfulness or meaning of Bible stories. In fact, reviewing chapter 1 is a good exercise at this point. The idea that the story of Cain embodies is that if we do not control the sin in our lives it will destroy us, but that abstract statement produces less impact on us than we experience when we relive the story and see how Cain plunges himself into greater and greater destruction as he refuses to master the monster sin in his life.

## How to Move from Story to Meaning

Our starting premise for moving from story to theme is that stories possess a discourse level as well as a purely narrative level. A synonym for discourse level is *message level*. A story exists to convey truth about living and not only to entertain us. Some of this truth is ideational, and the word that literary scholars use for the ideas in a work of literature is *theme(s)*.

The following discussion of methods of determining the themes of a Bible story will cover multiple ways of going about the task. These methods are somewhat overlapping. They achieve the goal of moving from story to meaning in different ways. To some degree we are free to choose a method from a menu of good options. Perhaps one method simply seems more natural or correct to you personally. Sometimes there is value in applying two methods to a story for the purpose of reinforcement or to uncover additional insights into a story. If you are the regular teacher of a class, you might wish to vary the methods as a way of avoiding monotony.

One other preliminary needs to be stated: the starting point for moving from story to meaning is to first interact with the story as a story. This chapter of the book covers activities in which we engage *after* we have done the types of analysis that the preceding chapters have outlined. Especially important is the process of identifying the action—dividing a story into units and naming them accurately. Doing this pays big dividends when we move from story to theme.

The format for the following discussion is to delineate the methods of moving from story to meaning first, and then apply them to the same text (the story of Abraham and Sarah's sojourn in the court of Pharaoh).

## *Bible Stories as Example Stories*

Every story is at some level an example story. This can apply either to characters in a story or the events and plot of a story. We need to turn a deaf ear to people who disparage this idea as being simplistic. This is simply how stories work, and the fact that the concept is easy to grasp is part of its usefulness.

The important question is of course what a given story is an example of. A story might be an example of multiple things. To lend analytic rigor and objectivity to the process of determining what a story is an example of, we need to identify the action (divide the story into units and name them accurately). Skipping this step is likely to land us in vagueness and leave us with impressions rather than verifiable conclusions. Having identified the action, we are in a good position to name what the story is an example of (and again it needs to be said that a story may be an example of more than one thing).

A further interpretive task is always part of this method, namely, the need to determine if a given example is a positive example to follow or a negative example to avoid. In arriving at that decision, we need to pay attention to the patterns of sympathy and aversion (approval and disapproval) that the story itself prompts in us. A story is a persuasive device on the part of the storyteller to get us to approve of some things and disapprove of others. We cannot move from story to meaning without engaging in this step of analysis.

## *Topic and Theme*

The framework of topic and theme is a time-tested method of moving from story to meaning. The *topic* of a story might be either an abstract concept or a universal human experience, and in fact those two are often indistinguishable. For example, the story of Abraham's willingness to sacrifice his son (Gen. 22:1–19) takes obedience to God as its subject (doing what God demands).

To be just a little more specific, the story of the offering of Isaac is a story of priorities, or of choosing obedience to God over all other values.

Having determined the subject or topic of a story, we need to formulate a statement of what the story says *about* that subject. What is the interpretive angle that the author and story have imposed on the subject of obeying God? What the story says about choosing obedience to God over all earthly values is that God rewards people who put him first. This is the theme of the story.

The framework of topic and theme is field tested and reliable. One thing to note about it is that it yields a somewhat simple version of a story, whereas other methods open the door to seeing more angles of vision. The framework of topic and theme results in a single focus for a story. In many situations this is a strength. It yields a high degree of clarity. That clarity gives way to confusion if we state more than one topic and theme for a story. Often the simple approach is the best approach, and in any case we never need to apologize for it.

### An Experiment in Living

It is in the nature of stories that the protagonist and sometimes other characters undertake an experiment in living. They adopt a scale of values and way of life. We can analyze what these are. It is entirely possible that for a given story we can identify multiple experiments in living, though we need to keep things relatively simple in order to avoid confusing ourselves or others.

Merely identifying a character's experiment in living does not yield an understanding of what a story is saying at the discourse level. Everything depends on whether the experiment in living succeeds or fails. Determining this requires analysis. Storytellers have *devices of disclosure* by which to guide our assessment of a character's experiment in living, including the following:

- *Outcome* is the most customary way in which storytellers tip their hands in regard to their intended message. Authors include data that gives a positive outcome or a negative outcome to the action. On the basis of that outcome, we reach a conclusion about what the story is saying about life.
- *Point of view* is another means by which a storyteller guides our response and understanding. A storyteller can simply include data that *disposes us* positively or negatively toward a character or action. In the story of the separation of Abraham and Lot (Gen. 13), we read twice that Abraham built an altar to God, with no corresponding mention of this for Lot. This disposes us to think that in the main action (choosing a place to live and ultimately a lifestyle), Abraham made the right choice.
- *Authorial commentary* is a means of disclosure that an author can use. To return to the story of the separation of Abraham and Lot, the author tells us flat out that the citizens of Sodom, where Lot chose to live, "were wicked, great sinners against the LORD" (Gen. 13:13). At that moment the storyteller asserts his viewpoint.

To return to the main point, we can move from story to meaning by identifying a character's experiment in living and then observing whether the story offers this experiment as something to practice or something to reject in our own lives.

### The World of the Story as a Picture of Reality

Our starting point here is that (in the words of novelist Joyce Cary) a storyteller always needs "some picture of the world, and of what is right and wrong in that world." To start with the first half of that statement, the world that we enter as we read a story is something that the author offers to us as an accurate picture of reality. If we identify the features of that world, we understand part of what the author wants us to accept as truth. The world of the story offers us a conception of what really exists and perhaps of what does not exist.

The second half of Joyce Cary's paradigm yields a further picture of the meaning of a story. A picture of what is right and wrong is a moral vision. Morality concerns a person's dealings with other people. What is "right" consists of a list of virtues. What is "wrong" is a list of vices. Every story puts characters in relation to other people, and it is usually possible to produce a list of what the story regards as virtues and a list of what it offers as vices.

### Summary Statement

Before we turn to an illustration of these methods of moving from story to meaning, we should let the point sink in that in large part these frameworks will yield a similar picture of what a story is asserting at the discourse or "message" level. In any case, we can do a good job of extracting the themes of a story if we choose any one of these methods. To review, those methods are (1) viewing the story as an example story, (2) determining the topic of a story (what it is about) and its theme (what it says *about* the chosen subject), (3) identifying the experiments in living and their outcome, and (4) analyzing the picture of the world in the story and what is right and wrong in that world. Additionally, identifying the human experiences portrayed in a story is part of the story's truth and meaning.

## From Story to Meaning in the Story of Abraham and Sarah's Sojourn in Egypt (Genesis 12:10–20)

As we turn now to a specimen story, we should remind ourselves that an adequate treatment of the story begins with an analysis of setting, characterization, and plot. Moving from story to meaning requires that we first interact with the story as a story. It is not the purpose of this chapter to perform that half of the equation.

> [10]Now there was a famine in the land. So Abram went down to Egypt to sojourn there, for the famine was severe in the land. [11]When he was about to enter Egypt, he said to Sarai his wife, "I know that you are a woman beautiful in appearance, [12]and when the Egyptians see you, they will say, 'This is his wife.' Then they will kill me, but they will let you live. [13]Say you are my sister, that it may go well with me because of you, and that my life may be spared for your sake." [14]When Abram entered Egypt, the Egyptians saw that the woman was very beautiful. [15]And when the princes of Pharaoh saw her, they praised her to Pharaoh. And the woman was taken into Pharaoh's house. [16]And for her sake he dealt well with Abram; and he had sheep, oxen, male donkeys, male servants, female servants, female donkeys, and camels.
>
> [17]But the LORD afflicted Pharaoh and his house with great plagues because of Sarai, Abram's wife. [18]So Pharaoh called Abram and said, "What is this you have done to me? Why did you not tell me that she was your wife? [19]Why did you say, 'She is my sister,' so that I took her for my wife? Now then, here is your wife; take her, and go." [20]And Pharaoh gave men orders concerning him, and they sent him away with his wife and all that he had.

Even though it is not the purpose of this chapter to conduct a full-scale narrative analysis of this story, the process of identifying the action is so necessary that we should take time to do it so we have that data before us. The sequence of this story is as follows: arrival → crisis/threat/danger → fear → expediency → rescue by divine intervention → escape from Egypt. The four methods out-lined above achieve the following results with this story:

- *An example story.* This story is an example of what happens when we resort to human ingenuity or expediency (doing what seems most immediately advantageous in dealing with a situation) instead of trusting in God's ability and willingness to protect us. It is an example of the negative effects of resorting to expediency instead of trust.

- *Topic and theme.* The subject or topic of this story can be formulated as "trusting in human ingenuity instead of God." The theme (what the story says *about* that subject) is that it is unwise and destructive to one's own interests to trust in human ingenuity instead of God.

- *An experiment in living.* Abraham and Sarah's experiment in living is to take matters into their own hands when they are confronted with a threat. The story does not offer an explicit negative verdict on that experiment. After all, Abraham and Sarah leave Egypt wealthier than they arrived. But we can infer that the experiment was not worth the risk.

- *A picture of the world and what is right and wrong in that world.* If the world of this story is a truthful picture of the world in which we live, what are we encouraged to believe is true of our world? The answers include the following: we live in a dangerous world that is capable of threatening our well-being; we need to make hard choices in that world; we make those choices, moreover, without knowing everything that it would be useful to know; a supernatural or spiritual world exists (the visible world is not the whole of reality); God's providential intervention exists and can work on our behalf. What constitutes good behavior in that world? Trusting in God; being truthful; respecting other people and not leaping to negative conclusions about them. What constitutes bad behavior? Trusting in human ingenuity to save us; being deceptive; maneuvering people to attain our own goals; not trusting God.

In regard to the foregoing, we should note the following things. First, it is obvious that all four approaches yield an accurate picture of the ideas embodied in the story of Abraham and Sarah. In each case we have successfully moved from story to meaning. Second, however, the four approaches are not identical. Some things emerge with more clarity with a given approach than with others. Third, in view of this, it is often advantageous to subject a story to two approaches rather than just one.

Finally, we cannot reach the conclusions stated above without answering the question, How do we know that Abraham made a bad decision when he lied to Pharaoh? Of what is Abraham guilty? If left to our intuitions, we might immediately say that we know Abraham did the wrong thing because he lied, but there are cases of legitimate civil disobedience (including deception) recorded in the Bible. Or we might be critical of Abraham because he misjudged the king's character, but that is a less than certain foundation for judging his experiment in living negatively. A reliable answer begins by identifying the action (see above). The key to assessing Abraham's decision is that God rescued him through divine intervention. In view of that, we judge Abraham's decision negatively because of his failure to trust God to deliver him.

## LEARNING BY DOING

The following application to the story of Ananias and Sapphira, to which we might give the title "A Day in the Life of the Early Church," appears in Acts 4:32–5:11. For the exercise to achieve its full effect, you need to commit yourself to not rushing the exercise and instead applying all four methods of moving from story to meaning. This will enable you to see what each of the four methods yields so you can employ them accordingly in the future. (In regard to the "world" of the story that we enter as we read it, an important feature of that world is that the earthly sphere exists within a larger spiritual realm in which God sees what people do and in which miraculous events happen.)

> [4:32]Now the full number of those who believed were of one heart and soul, and no one said that any of the things that belonged to him was his own, but they had everything in common. [33]And with great power the apostles were giving their testimony to the resurrection of the Lord Jesus, and great grace was upon them all. [34]There was not a needy person among them, for as many as were owners of lands or houses sold them and brought the proceeds of what was sold [35]and laid it at the apostles' feet, and it was distributed to each as any had need. [36]Thus Joseph, who was also called by the apostles Barnabas (which means son of encouragement), a Levite, a native of Cyprus, [37]sold a field that belonged to him and brought the money and laid it at the apostles' feet.
>
> [5:1]But a man named Ananias, with his wife Sapphira, sold a piece of property, [2]and with his wife's knowledge he kept back for himself some of the proceeds and brought only

a part of it and laid it at the apostles' feet. ³But Peter said, "Ananias, why has Satan filled your heart to lie to the Holy Spirit and to keep back for yourself part of the proceeds of the land? ⁴While it remained unsold, did it not remain your own? And after it was sold, was it not at your disposal? Why is it that you have contrived this deed in your heart? You have not lied to man but to God." ⁵When Ananias heard these words, he fell down and breathed his last. And great fear came upon all who heard of it. ⁶The young men rose and wrapped him up and carried him out and buried him.

⁷After an interval of about three hours his wife came in, not knowing what had happened. ⁸And Peter said to her, "Tell me whether you sold the land for so much." And she said, "Yes, for so much." ⁹But Peter said to her, "How is it that you have agreed together to test the Spirit of the Lord? Behold, the feet of those who have buried your husband are at the door, and they will carry you out." ¹⁰Immediately she fell down at his feet and breathed her last. When the young men came in they found her dead, and they carried her out and buried her beside her husband. ¹¹And great fear came upon the whole church and upon all who heard of these things.

## Final Thoughts on Moving from Story to Meaning

We should begin by noting that there is no single right way to extract the ideas from a story. We have multiple good options available to us. We personally might feel more comfortable with some of the methods than with others. Or a given story might lend its meanings better to one approach rather than another.

Given the four options, we cannot make a bad choice, regardless of what it is.

Second, it is impossible to overstress the point that moving from story to meaning is ordinarily *the last thing* that we do with a Bible story. Our first task is to relive the story as vividly as possible. Then we need to name the recognizable human experiences that a story embodies and gets us to see clearly, realizing that this is a level of truth or meaning in the story. Formulating the themes of the story ordinarily comes last.

Third, this means that we should not be in a hurry to get to the religious or moral ideas in a Bible story. If we fast forward to the ideational level, we will short circuit the richness that the story stands ready to give us at other levels, and we even stand a good chance of not getting the ideas quite right because we have not assimilated the story fully. In much biblical scholarship, preaching, and Bible study, there is too much time or space devoted to the ideas of Bible stories and not enough time or space to reliving the story and absorbing the human experiences that are silhouetted with heightened clarity in it.

Finally, for two additional angles on moving from story to meaning, I offer the following quotations by famous literary authors; I have used their formulas to good effect as supplementary alternatives to the four methods I develop earlier in this chapter. Nineteenth-century French writer Charles Baudelaire said that storytellers gravitate to stories "in which the deep significance of life reveals itself." We can thus ask, What is the deep significance of life that this story embodies and clarifies?

T. S. Eliot wrote that "it is the function of all art to give us some perception of an order in life, by imposing an order upon it." The "content question" that we can ask is, What perception of an order in life do I receive when reading this story? The "literary form question" is, What order has the storyteller imposed on the materials of life? Chapters 2–7 of this book have explored the types of order that a storyteller imposes on the materials of life. The concluding chapter has in effect explored the subject of the perception of life that a story imparts.